MATH HACKS

COOL TIPS + LESS STRESS = BETTER MARKS!

Vanessa "The Math Guru" Vakharia

Illustrations by Hyein Lee

Scholastic Canada Ltd.
Toronto New York London Auckland Sydney
Mexico City New Delhi Hong Kong Buenos Aires

This book is dedicated to anyone, myself included, who's been fooled by the myth that there is such a thing as a "math person." If an ex-math-hater like me can see the light, then anyone can.

This book would not exist if it weren't for all of the very special humans who believe in me, always, no matter what. Thank you for being you and for knowing what I need when even I don't know what I need. Which is often. An extra special thank you to: Sarah Bartram, Wendy Bircher, Sandra Birkett, Stefanie Bradley, Imogen Coe, Lindsay Coppens, Aldo Fierro, the Gibsons, Emily Gottschalk, Erin Haggett, Eva Kasinska, Karina Keeble, David Kochberg, Simon Kwan, Maral Maclagan, Erin O'Connor, Joanna Perlmutar, the Pirbhais, the Prusskys, Brooke Ramsay, Sabrina Stolski, Heather Tormey, Nadia Vakharia and Selene Vakharia, as well as every student, parent, and tutor that has been part of The Math Guru community and who make everything mean everything.

— Vanessa Vakharia

Scholastic Canada Ltd.
604 King Street West, Toronto, Ontario M5V 1E1, Canada

Scholastic Inc.
557 Broadway, New York, NY 10012, USA

Scholastic Australia Pty Limited
PO Box 579, Gosford, NSW 2250, Australia

Scholastic New Zealand Limited
Private Bag 94407, Botany, Manukau 2163, New Zealand

Scholastic Children's Books
Euston House, 24 Eversholt Street, London NW1 1DB, UK

www.scholastic.ca

Library and Archives Canada Cataloguing in Publication
Vakharia, Vanessa, author
Math hacks : cool tips + less stress = better marks / Vanessa
Vakharia ; illustrated by Hyein Lee.

ISBN 978-1-4431-6316-3 (softcover)

1. Mathematics--Juvenile literature. I. Lee, Hyein, illustrator
II. Title.

QA40.5.V34 2018   j510   C2018-900644-7

6 5 4 3 2 1   Printed in Malaysia 108   18 19 20 21 22

Table of Contents

THE BEST MATH BOOK IN THE WORLD!

Who even am I and why did I write this in the first place?

Me, grade 5. The only thing crazier than my hair was that I thought I was not a math person.

Me, now! I am TOTALLY a math person, sing in a band, run my own business and do other cool stuff!

Great question! I'll start by telling you a secret — I failed math in high school. TWICE!!! Yep . . . that happened. Now I'm a math teacher and an entrepreneur. I started one of the coolest tutoring studios ever, where we teach math and science to hundreds of kids just like you. It's in Toronto and it's called The Math Guru!

When I was younger, I didn't really love math so much. I didn't understand it, it stressed me out and it wasn't fun to do. It's hard to enjoy something if you feel like you're no good at it, and that's exactly how I felt.

One day, a teacher explained math to me in a way I had never heard anyone explain it. It was like this crazy cool light bulb went on in my head — POOF — just like that!

And all of a sudden I realized: *Hey, I'm not bad at math AT ALL! I just never heard it explained the right way for ME!* My whole life changed after that. Not only did I realize that math is actually SO cool once you get it, but the whole thing taught me that anyone can do math. Sometimes all it takes is the right teacher or the right book.

I don't want you to think you can't do math, because I know that's not true (even if YOU don't know it yet). And if you can do math — even if you've spent your entire life thinking you can't — well, that means that you can do ANYTHING IN THE WHOLE WIDE WORLD!

And that's why I wrote this book.

How should YOU use this book?

So straight up, you go ahead and use this book however you want to. You do you! But here are a few tips to get the most out of it:

#1: Let's be friends! Can we please? But for real, when you're reading this book, picture ME (a happy, smiley, chill person) doing math with YOU, just like a friend!

#2: It's okay to jump around! You totally don't have to read it in order! Just flip to the section that you need and go from there! No need to spend time reading stuff you already get!

#3: Don't sweat all the stuff! I obviously couldn't fit EVERY single math thing in this book, because it would be ginormous! But most of the major stuff that kids in grades 3–6 find hard or get stuck on is in here — and that's a lot! There is also extra stuff at **www.scholastic.ca/mathhacks**, so be sure to check there too.

#4: You do you! If you understand something a different way than I've explained it, that's totally okay! Everyone learns differently and that's what makes us each special and amazing. I've explained stuff in a way that I find most kids understand, but YOU pick the way YOU get it best!

#5: Do the examples with me! Every single section has examples that are fully worked out. Once you think you get it, write out the example question and try to do the WHOLE thing yourself without looking at the answer. Then check to see if you got it right . . . and if not, retrace your steps to see where you went wrong, and try again! This is a great way to make sure that you totally understand each concept before moving on.

YOU HACK YOU!

HEALTH HACKS

Take care of the most important person — YOU!

Sometimes we're so focused on working hard that we forget to take care of ourselves. What does that have to do with being good at math? We need our brains working properly to be good at math, right? And our brains live in our bodies. Being physically tired or hungry or feeling yucky can make learning math way harder than it actually is — trust me, I've been there! I've stayed up waaaay too late studying for a test and forgotten to eat properly or even brush my teeth! The next day, even though I knew my stuff, I didn't do so well. I didn't have enough energy to power my brain. So, here are some hacks that will TOTALLY make your brain's home the best place EVER! Doing things over and over helps you build habits. That's true for math and other things in life too.

#1: Catch some zzzzz's! It may sound a bit boring, but sleep is THE most important thing for brain function. If you're tired, not only will you be grumpy, but you won't be able to think as well as you normally would. It's more important for you to get a good night's sleep than it is to stay up really late studying. Make sure you stick to your bedtime and turn off the lights when you're supposed to. Plus, math — and school and EVERYTHING! — will be ten times more fun if you aren't grumpy.

#2: Make nighttime the best time Create a routine that helps you relax and get ready for a good sleep. Shut down those screens at least an hour before bedtime (for reals!) and start to chill. I like having a bubble bath, drinking some tea and then reading in bed. Figure out what makes you feel relaxed and ready for bed, and do it EVERY NIGHT. You'll look forward to bedtime and you'll be so much happier the next day.

#3: Don't skip breakfast You know how everyone says that breakfast is the most important meal of the day? Well, it's true! Imagine if you didn't put gas in a car and then expected it just to run. Duh! That wouldn't work. Your brain is like that too. For it to go properly, you have to charge it up first. If you're not hungry first thing in the morning, make a smoothie to go, and pack it with everything you need to get your brain ready to rock.

#4: Snack smart So, breakfast is totally important, but your brain needs boosts all day long. Make sure your backpack is full of healthy little snacks that you can munch on throughout the day. And it matters WHAT you put in your body. We all love candy and junk food, but they actually make us more tired. Save them for weekends or times when you don't need your brain to be focused.

#5: Don't run dry One of the MAIN reasons that people get tired and grumpy throughout the day is because they're thirsty ... and don't even know it. It's true! Think of yourself as a plant that needs to be watered regularly. Get a cool water bottle (one that doesn't leak!) and stick it in your backpack. Before and after recess and at lunch, have a few big gulps of water, whether you think you're thirsty or not. Water your brain and see how much better you feel!

RELAX HACKS

Enough with the freak-out — chill out instead!

You know what makes freaking out scary? Feeling like you're the only one freaking out! But here's a secret: everyone freaks out sometimes. I used to freak out about math all the time, until I learned how to chill and be okay with not understanding everything at first. I even freaked out a bit while I was writing this book (LOL!), because some of it was really, really hard to do. But I got through it and so can YOU. Freaking out is just a part of life, and it won't last forever — the trick is to learn to deal when it happens. And there are lots of things you can do to calm down, get focused and be ready to go!

#1: Just BREATHE If you're freaking out 'cause you can't figure something out and you're about to go nuts — you need to breathe. Not like you normally breathe. You need to focus on it, like this:

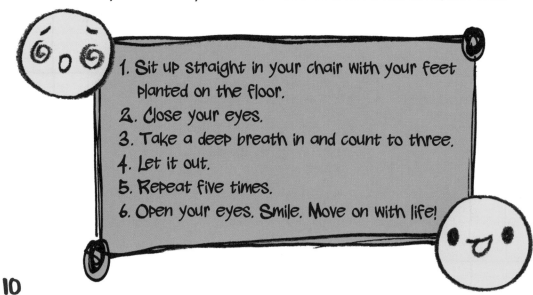

1. Sit up straight in your chair with your feet planted on the floor.
2. Close your eyes.
3. Take a deep breath in and count to three.
4. Let it out.
5. Repeat five times.
6. Open your eyes. Smile. Move on with life!

#2: Get a grip   If there's a math question you just CAN'T get and you're like, "OMG this is the end of the world!" well, it's time to get a grip. What do I mean? I want you to think about WHY you're freaking out. So what, you don't understand something — what's the big deal? You know what learning is? It's NOT understanding something and working hard until you DO. That might take a minute, an hour, a day, a week, even a month. And that's okay. Just relax . . . eventually you'll get it. Really! Try to be patient and remember that not understanding is a key part of learning. If you already knew everything, life would be sooo boring.

#3: Sharing is caring   You know what the worst thing to do is? Keep all the stress, worry and frustration bottled up inside. It makes you feel like you're about to explode, and that's a yucky feeling. If you're freaking out, or sad, or scared, or stressed, or just super down for no reason at all — talk to someone! Call a friend! Tell your dad or your grandma, a teacher, or even your dog! It can feel kind of scary to say this stuff out loud, but just say the words "hey, I'm freaking out right now" and it will feel like a huge weight is off your shoulders.

#4: Body scan This is one of my favourite things to do when I'm freaking out. What you're going to do is this: Stop what you're doing. If you're doing homework, stop. If you're writing a test, just stop for a second. This doesn't take long and can make such a difference! So, STOP and:

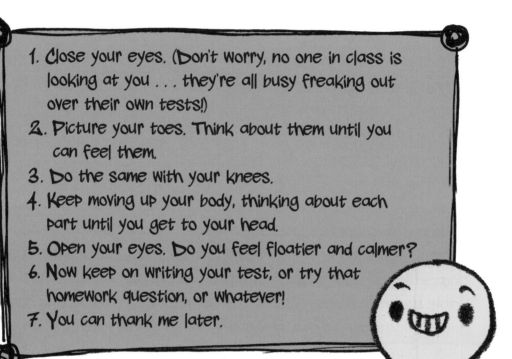

1. Close your eyes. (Don't worry, no one in class is looking at you . . . they're all busy freaking out over their own tests!)
2. Picture your toes. Think about them until you can feel them.
3. Do the same with your knees.
4. Keep moving up your body, thinking about each part until you get to your head.
5. Open your eyes. Do you feel floatier and calmer?
6. Now keep on writing your test, or try that homework question, or whatever!
7. You can thank me later.

#5: Start a freak-out journal A what? It's like a diary, but one that you write in when you feel stressed. No one else gets to read it unless you want them to. Get yourself a notebook that you love and a cool pen. When you're feeling overwhelmed, grab it and write down why. You'll find that the more you write this stuff down, the less scary it becomes. It's a way to share something with your best friend ever — yourself!

#6: Brain vacation Have you been staring at a question forever and you just CAN'T figure it out and you're starting to lose it? Get up and leave the math problem behind for a few minutes. When your brain is stuck it can't work like it normally does. Go for a walk, take a shower, play with your cat — do anything as long as your mind gets a mini-vacation. When you get back to your work, you'll be able to look at it in a whole new way.

#7: Build your chill-out muscles The more you deal with your freak-outs head-on, the less power they will have over you. Think about it: Imagine you went to the gym and tried to lift fifty pounds. That would be impossible, right? But what if you started by lifting five pounds every day. Then moved to ten … then fifteen … and so on. Eventually, you would be able to lift a lot! Building your chill-out muscles works the exact same way. If you use these hacks, your freak-outs will seem less and less scary. Later, when you have bigger tests — and even exams one day — you'll be totally able to deal because your chill-out muscles will be strong and ready to tackle anything!

SUPERSTAR HACKS

For when you feel like maybe you DON'T got this . . .

Being good at math is only partly about the actual math. A huge part of it has to do with feeling great about YOURSELF. If you feel like a superstar, you're more likely to believe that you can do anything — even math. So, for sure, do your math homework, but do your superstar homework too! That means reading this whole section and using the hacks ASAP. The sooner you realize what a STAR you are, the sooner you'll start loving math — and your whole life too!

#1: Make FAIL your friend Every single person you think is cool has experienced failure, like, a ton of times. You NEED to make mistakes, bomb tests and get it wrong to actually succeed. What? Failure exists so that you can learn and get better at stuff and become a stronger person. It can seem embarrassing to fail, especially when you've worked hard. But take a second right now to think about something that you got wrong at first. Tying your shoe? Riding a bike? I bet the first time you tried it, you failed. And now you don't even care because you're kicking butt at it. Math is like that too! You might struggle and get things wrong. You might fail a test. But what matters is that you keep trying. Use failure to motivate yourself to do better!

It's OK!

#2: Don't compare yourself to others   You know that kid in class who magically gets everything while you have to do so much work to get it? Here's a secret: that kid has to work hard at other things — you just don't know it. I bet there are things that you find super easy that some of your friends struggle with. That's just how it goes! We're all different. But you know what makes people superstars? When they work hard at the things that AREN'T so easy. Anyone can do the easy stuff! Real superstars try the hard stuff too. And often they're not perfect at it right away. So, if math is tough for you, you're already a step closer to becoming a superstar, because here you are, trying and refusing to give up. Give yourself a high-five — you've got this!

#3: You are what YOU say you are   Every morning after I get out of bed, I look in the mirror and say out loud, "Good morning, Vanessa! Guess what? YOU ARE A SUPERSTAR!" Yep, I actually do that. Sometimes I make funny faces, flex my muscles, jump up and down — whatever it takes for me to get pumped up. It reminds me that I'm awesome, and if I start feeling bummed out during the day, I just think of my mirror moment. You can do this too! And if you're doing homework and start getting the blahs, find a mirror and do it again! You will seriously feel better right away. So, tell yourself what a superstar you are, every single day.

#4: You're smarter than you think   Ever notice that sometimes you spend a lot of time complaining about the bad stuff? Like, you totally forget about the amazingness that happens every day. It's the same when we think about ourselves. Instead of remembering all of the things we're awesome at, we focus on the things that we're not good at yet. When you do that, it's easy to start thinking that you're bad at everything. The truth is that there are just a few things you're not great at YET — but there's a whole bunch of things you ARE great at RIGHT NOW! For reals, do this now: Take a piece of paper and divide it into two sections, one for "Things I Am Awesome At" and the other for "Things I Find Hard." Do your lists. Be honest and put down anything you think of. Ask a family member or friend to help you think of things too. Now tell me, which list is bigger? The awesome side, right?

AWESOME
drawing
baking cookies
backflips
stuffie collection
science experiments
anything Super Mario
jokes

HARD
cleaning my room
fractions
waking up

#5: Be your own best friend Think about your best friend for a second. Can you think of a million good things about that person? I bet you can! So why, when we think about ourselves, are we so much meaner than we would ever be to our friends? The next time you're thinking mean thoughts about yourself, ask yourself, "Hey, would I say this stuff about my best friend?" If the answer is "NO WAY!" then don't say it about yourself either. Because being your own best friend is pretty cool.

#6: We ALL have bad days Feeling bummed because today you just weren't getting it, no matter how hard you tried? Hey, it's okay! You are going to have both kinds of days, good and bad. That's called BALANCE — and it's a good thing! Sure, we would love for it to be nice out all the time, but it has to rain sometimes too. After the rain, we love a sunny day that much more. So, if you're having a bad day, remember that it isn't forever. Soon you'll have a GREAT day, and when it comes, it will be that much better!

#7: Marks aren't everything How often do you get down on yourself because you didn't do so well on a test or because so-and-so got a better mark than you? Here's a secret: it's not about the marks. Sure, marks are important and it's cool to have goals, but the real measure of success is PROGRESS. Here's how progress works: Say you're so-so with fractions. You study hard and take your test, but when you get your test back, you didn't do as well as you hoped . . . total disappointment. But you should be proud! You worked hard and learned things you didn't know before. Maybe this time you weren't as nervous about doing the test as you've been in the past. And maybe you even did a tiny bit better than last time. Any of these things means that you are doing AWESOME — you are making progress! Eventually your marks will start improving. You just have to be patient and start celebrating ALL of your accomplishments, not just your marks.

HACK YOUR LEARNING STYLE

Figure out how to look at math YOUR way!

Knowing how YOU learn best is one of the secrets to acing math. Sometimes it takes a while to figure it out, but once you do, BINGO!

There are three main types of learners: People who learn best by seeing things are **visual learners**. People who learn best by touching things are **tactile learners**. And people who learn best by hearing things are **auditory learners**. The best part? You can be more than one kind! Many people have a combo of learning styles and it can be good to mix it up, especially if you get stuck. Check out the categories to see where you fit!

Hacks for Visual Learners

Do you like drawing pictures? Do you remember things better if there are diagrams or you see them written out on the board? Do you like to doodle? Do you learn stuff better if it's written on a piece of paper instead of if someone just tells it to you? If you answered YES to some of these questions, then you might be a visual learner. And if you are, here are some ways you can max out your visual-learning powers.

#1: Write everything down I can't remember anything without writing it down. And when I don't — POOF! — it's gone. Even when I swear I will remember it. So, I write down everything I need to know. Write stuff down in class, even if no one else does. And when you're studying for tests, write things down on a piece of paper. You will totally understand and remember them better!

#2: Use lots of colours Highlight everything! Invent your own colour-coding system for your math notes. Use bright sticky notes to mark stuff you have to remember, and get cool stickers to put by important notes. Using colours is key for visual learners because colours help their brains organize information. So, grab a pack of markers and start making your math notes as colourful as a rainbow slushy.

#3: Draw diagrams Visual learners usually remember pictures, so turn everything into a diagram and memorize that. If you have a list of math rules, put bubbles around them and use arrows to point to examples. There are tons of types of diagrams, so be creative and invent a system that works for you.

#4: Use your imagination If the question is about fractions, imagine a yummy pizza sliced into a bunch of pieces. If the lesson is about spheres, picture a giant basketball or a jawbreaker. If it's perimeter, think about building a fence. Use your imagination to turn math concepts into pictures and stories and you'll find it so much easier to remember stuff.

Hacks for Tactile Learners

Do you move around a lot? Do you start getting antsy if you're sitting still for too long? Do you like building things? Do you like to take things apart to see how they work? Do you learn better while doing actual activities? If you answered yes to some of these questions, then you might be a tactile learner, and these hacks will totally help you out.

#1: Stay busy If you have trouble sitting still and focusing, keep your hands busy. This time, it's fine to fidget! Try putty or modelling clay — you can mash it in one hand while you write with the other. Chewing gum can totally help. Or tapping your foot. Anything you can do to keep your body busy so your brain can pay attention can help — just make sure you're not bugging your classmates.

#2: Math in action Experiencing math in the real world is the best. Empty your piggy bank and count it up. Do chores or odd jobs to earn money, and keep track of how much you save and spend. Be a future millionaire! Tag along to the grocery store and weigh things on the scales in the fruit and veggie section. Using math concepts in the REAL world will help you understand them. Then you'll be ready to ace your real homework.

#3: Make stuff Whenever possible, make something! If you're having trouble with 3-D shapes, grab some paper and tape and make a model. If you're having trouble with multiplication, use mini-marshmallows and put them into groups so you can see what's going on. (Bonus: you can eat your work!) So, touch some actual stuff and move it around!

Hacks for Auditory Learners

Do you like talking to people, like, a lot? Do you prefer when someone just tells you what to do instead of having to read instructions? Are skits and presentations more fun than written assignments? Do you like to speak up in class? Do you talk to yourself? If you answered yes to some of these questions, you might be an auditory learner, so listen up!

#1: Talk to yourself   So, first make sure you're not bothering anyone around you, and if you're cool, then feel free to talk to yourself! Read those math questions out loud. Explain how you're going to solve them. When you write out your steps, SAY them. Talking out loud can help auditory learners fully understand what's going on, so make some noise!

#2: Partner up   If you're like me, you learn so much better when you're working with a friend. Pair up with a pal and take turns explaining math concepts to each other. Do math questions together and brainstorm different ways to get the answer. Talking to a friend really, really helps — and it's fun!

#3: Repeat after me   If you get confused in class, raise that hand and ask your teacher to repeat what they just said. Just asking your question out loud will help you understand things better. Even auditory learners sometimes need to hear things a few times before those things stick in their head, so go ahead and ask for a replay.

CLASS HACKS

It's YOUR class time — use it well!

Sometimes it can feel like math class is this big, confusing circus and you don't know where to look or what to do or how to enjoy it! Use these ideas to help get the most from your class time. I mean, circuses can be FUN once you stop being scared of clowns, right?

#1: Get front-row seats! Just like when you go to a concert, the front row is where it's at. If you're sitting at the front of the classroom, it's so much easier to pay attention. You can see the board better, you won't get distracted by other kids so much (because you can't see them!) and you'll be able to hear your teacher more easily AND see the board better. If you're not already sitting at the front, ask your teacher if you can move. It's a small thing that will make a BIG difference.

#2: Shhhhh! When your teacher's talking, you should be listening — and doing nothing else. Lessons move FAST, and if you're chatting with a friend or doodling, you're going to miss something. And if you miss one little thing, even for a second, the rest of the lesson might not make sense. So, save it for after the bell.

#3: Avoid the class clowns I love funny people just as much as you do — who doesn't? But it's super hard to concentrate when you're surrounded by talking, laughing people. Save your friends for recess and pick a quiet seat for class. You'll be able to focus better, and you'll get so much more from the lesson.

#4: Ask questions It can be scary to feel like you don't know what's going on. But asking your teacher to explain something is sooo much better than sitting there feeling confused. The other kids will probably be thankful that you had the guts to put your hand up, because they were too nervous to ask. Stand up for yourself, tell your teacher what you need, and be the hero the rest of your class is secretly looking for.

#5: Listen for clues I learned this one when I was in school: the lesson is only half of the ACTUAL lesson. Sometimes your teacher will give you clues about what's important or what might show up on a test. If they spend a lot of time on a concept or question, it probably means that it's super important. If your teacher's all "I LOVE this question so much!" it's a hint that a question like that will be on your next test. Be a detective and listen for clues. When you hear one, write it down so that you can remember it when you're studying later.

#6: Explore your classroom   Your class can be a treasure chest of things that can help you do math better. Is there a secret stash of books you can use? Math games you can play? Models you can build? School supplies to help organize your binder and make your notes easier to read? Ask your teacher what you can get your hands on . . . and use it!

#7: Make a questions sheet   Sometimes there's a lot to understand and you can't get it all at once. So, have a "special questions for later" page ready for every class. If you don't get something that your teacher is explaining, make a quick note like "What do I do with remainders?" After the lesson, you can ask your teacher to explain it to you again, or ask a friend or parent after school. That way you'll get all the info you need.

#8: Always play catch-up   If you miss class, don't sweat it . . . but DO catch up on the lesson. Ask your teacher what you missed. Get worksheets or practice questions and do them right away. You need to stay on top of your math game every day!

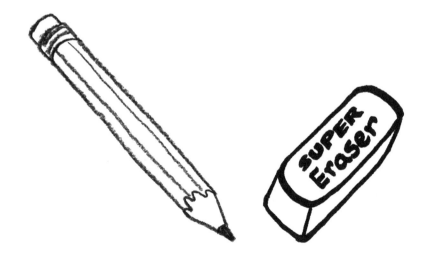

MEMORY HACKS

Yes, you CAN memorize anything!

I know you're probably rolling your eyes right now. No one likes to memorize stuff, okay? But if you want to be good at math there are certain things you NEED to memorize. Like your times tables! You need both understanding and memorization to rock math. But there is good news: memorizing stuff doesn't have to suck. Try as many of these tricks as it takes until one of them works for you. And if you don't use it, you lose it! That means you've gotta keep going over stuff until you know it in your sleep, so don't sweat it.

#1: Break it up You can chill — no one's asking you to memorize, like, ALL of your times tables in one day. If your school gave you an agenda, use it to come up with a plan! Day 1, work on your 3 times table. The next day, it's on to the 4s. The day after that, do 3s and 4s. Keep on going until you know everything. Working on memory stuff for just ten minutes a day can turn you into a TOTAL PRO in a month. So get started — now!

#2: Get an app Is gaming your thing? There are loads of cool apps out there to help you memorize math. You'll barely even notice that you're learning as you try to beat your high score. Ask your teacher which ones might be good, or get a parent to go to an app store, search the subjects you need to work on, and download away. Play ten minutes a day and win at math!

#3: Time for timers Some kids get stressed when they see a timer, but timers can actually make math memory stuff go faster! Set your timer . . . How many times can you write the 8 times table over and over in five minutes? In one minute? This is even MORE fun when you do it with a friend.

#4: Invent a game Sometimes memorizing is boring. But you know what is fun? Games! Get creative and turn your fave game into a math game. Make a deck of multiplication cards and play memory. Grab some chalk and make a giant hopscotch court on your sidewalk, and fill each square with math facts. You won't even notice that you're doing work.

#5: Bust a rhyme You know how a song will get stuck in your head without you even trying to memorize it? Music and rhyme are magic. Take your fave song and change the words so that they're all about whatever it is you have to memorize! Or go freestyle and make your own slam-style rhymes.

6 times 6 is 36, that's my multiplication trick
6 times 7 is 42, cats go meow and cows go moo
6 times 8 is 48, now let's go out and roller skate

#6: Flash cards for EVERYTHING I love flash cards! You know those ones with questions on the front and answers on the back? They're perfect for memorizing things. For example, cut some paper into cards and write "8 x 2" on the front of a card and the answer (16!) on the back. Do this for all of your times tables or whatever it is you need to remember. Look at the question. Do you know it? Flip it over to see if you're right! Put the ones you struggle with in a "struggle pile" and keep at them until you've got it.

#7: Use a funny voice Repeating things can work really well to get them to stick in your head. Try using different voices every time you say it. Use a British accent, an opera singer voice, a whisper, a robot voice, a celeb voice, whatever! Improv with a friend and see who can come up with the best voice.

#8: Make a story Come up with a crazy story that involves whatever you're trying to memorize. Say that's multiplying positive and negative numbers. It's a robot battle! When two good (positive!) robots face off, they don't even fight because they are that nice. So, that battle equals nobody getting hurt (positive outcome/answer). Then it's two evil (negative!) robots. But all the negativity causes them to short circuit and nobody gets hurt (positive outcome/answer). But when it's a good robot vs. an evil robot, the battle happens and stuff gets wrecked. So, that's not good (negative outcome/answer).

Wanna get started?

There are Math Guru–approved lists of cool math apps, examples of games to play, rockin' rhymes and more at **www.scholastic.ca/math-hacks**

FEELING STUCK!

Hacks for when you just can't seem to get it :(

Sometimes no matter how hard you try to understand something, you just can't seem to get it. Or you study hard for a test, and when it starts, you just go blank. Sometimes you feel like math is never going to get any easier. It's normal to feel all of those things. These hacks are for you, and they WILL make you feel better.

#1: Change it up Everyone's brain is totally different. Like, you and your best friend both love ice cream, but you don't like the same flavours. The same is true with math. There is one correct answer, but sometimes there are different ways to get there. Say a fraction question is stumping you. Erase everything you know about it and ask a friend or parent to explain it. They may think of fractions in a slightly different way — one that may make more sense to you.

#2: Get online You might have the most awesome teacher on the planet, but sometimes lessons just don't click in class. There are tons of websites that can teach you the same subject, but in a slightly different way. Videos can be an easy way to learn math. Ask a grown-up for some help and get online. All you have to do is type your topic into any search engine, see which vids pop up, and watch and learn.

#3: Talk it out Seriously, sit down with someone and just start talking. Tell them about the problem you're stuck on. What does it say? Why is it confusing? What were you learning in class when this problem popped up? Those could be hints about what you're supposed to do. Once you start talking, you may feel a giant light bulb POP on in your head. And if you don't see a light bulb, maybe your friend will have an idea for you to try.

#4: Ask your teacher This is SUCH a good idea — obviously they will know what to do, right?! Make an appointment and treat this meeting like a pro. Write down your questions beforehand and make notes about where and why you're feeling stuck. That way when you show up, your teacher will know exactly what you want help with, and you will get exactly the help you need.

#5: Go backwards Not remembering something they're supposed to have already learned is one of the main reasons kids feel stuck. Math is like a giant building where topics stack on top of one another like bricks. Say you're doing column addition and you forget your addition facts? Column addition would be hard to do! You need to figure out the little bricks you are missing. Then get some help with those and get ready to build up, up and UP!

#6: Did you miss out? Are you staring at your homework feeling like "Umm . . . is this from Mars?" First of all — did you miss something? Were you in class the day the lesson was taught? Do you have all of the worksheets and notes that your teacher handed out? If you were away, you WILL get stuck, so chase down what you missed. Talk to your teacher after being away and borrow some notes from a friend. Get yourself caught up, every single time.

#7: Find your question's twin If you're stuck on a homework question, there's a good chance there's another one that's sort of the same, only with different numbers — your question's twin. Did your teacher do one like it in class? What did your teacher do to solve that problem? Maybe you can use the same strategy to answer yours.

HOMEWORK HACKS

Make homework actually work for you!

Okay so, no one LOVES homework, but it's just something you've gotta do to get where you want to be. The less time you spend complaining about it, the faster you will get it done. And while you're at it, you might as well make it awesome and be proud of your work. Go get 'em, homework tiger!

#1: Pencils are your BFF Making mistakes is a part of math. It's going to happen, so be prepared . . . and use a pencil. You're going to need to do things over and over again, so forget the pen. Have a good eraser handy and take as many do-overs as you want.

#2: Build a homework habit Have you ever heard that it takes a month to build a habit? It's true. Try doing your homework at the same time every single day. That way your brain and body get used to it, and when homework time comes along, they'll be totally ready to go.

#3: Find your study sweet spot Having a special place to get in the study zone really helps. Find somewhere quiet where you can spread out your books, calculator and writing supplies. But not your bed. That's for sleeping! Do your work in your sweet spot ALL the time. You'll get into brain-activation mode way faster.

#4: Make a master plan "Master plan" sounds like a villain thing, but sometimes you'll have regular homework, a test to study for AND an assignment due in a few days. That can be hard to manage! After school, make a list of everything you have to do that night. Use a checklist and cross each item off after you've completed it. Remember to take breaks in between each thing.

#5: Trouble? Ask your teacher See your teacher the day after you've had homework trouble, and ask them to help you. They know the material best. If you figure it out RIGHT away, you won't have trouble later when you see it on a test.

#6: Study buddies are the best Sometimes I hated doing homework because I was all like, "*Wahhh!* All of my friends are somewhere having fun without me!" But they were all doing homework too — I just didn't know it. Studying with friends can be fun and super-helpful, as long as you follow some rules. First, no talking until break time. Second, you can be working on different things as long as you're all doing homework. Third, save the snacks for later — they're distracting and messy. But when break time hits, make sure you have good ones ready to go.

#7: Make a homework magic kit Take the time to make your homework super YOU. You 100% need some good pencils, highlighters, markers, a cool binder, stickers, duct tape — all that great stuff! Your school or local library may have fun supplies you can use to dress up your work. It makes homework more creative, and when you need to study for a test, your notes will be so much nicer to look at.

#8: Take a break. You deserve it! Don't try to do ALL of your homework at once — you'll go nuts! Even a big brain gets tired after a while, so plan to take breaks. Use an alarm so you're not checking the clock. After twenty minutes or so — BING — break time! Use your break well. Get up, stretch, make a snack, dance around like crazy, call a friend, hop in the shower, do some jumping jacks — basically, do anything totally unrelated to school. After ten or fifteen minutes, you'll be recharged and ready to concentrate again.

#9: Reward yourself Make a deal with yourself: After you do ALL of your homework, you get to watch an episode of your favourite show. Or have dessert, or call a friend. Whatever motivates you, make that your reward so that there's a pot of gold at the end of your homework rainbow.

#10: Take the superstar approach If you don't have any official math homework, use the bonus time to go over something you had trouble with earlier. Redo those questions you didn't get, talk to a friend about a confusing concept, or have a do-over on an old quiz. Doing just a tiny bit more than what your teacher expects is a big way to stay on track to math SUPERSTARDOM.

#11: Find your focus! Can't concentrate? Feeling fidgety? It's easy to get distracted by your own thoughts: "Maybe I should get a snack? Or go to the washroom! Or get a glass of water . . . GAH!" Use these three top-secret focus tricks:

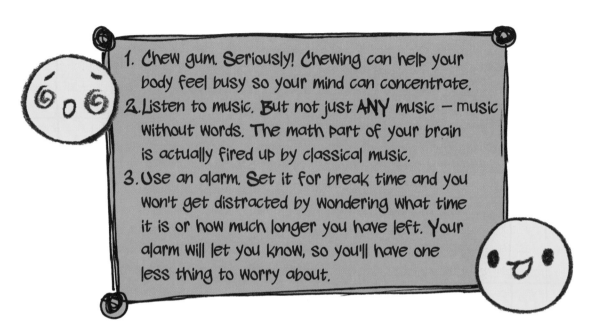

1. Chew gum. Seriously! Chewing can help your body feel busy so your mind can concentrate.
2. Listen to music. But not just ANY music — music without words. The math part of your brain is actually fired up by classical music.
3. Use an alarm. Set it for break time and you won't get distracted by wondering what time it is or how much longer you have left. Your alarm will let you know, so you'll have one less thing to worry about.

#12: Neat and tidy wins the race Make your homework look sharp! Neat work will score you more marks in class and be easier for you to study from when it's test time. Make sure your papers are organized. Use a folder, dividers, a ruler, colours, highlighters — whatever works for you. Being proud of your work is what will help you get ahead the most. You deserve it!

GOOD WORK

STUDY HACKS

Get ready to kill that test!

What does the word "study" even mean? Some kids think it's good enough to just read over their notes, hoping the info will magically stick in their brains. But that's not how it works. Imagine you just stared at a soccer ball for an hour and then were like, "There, I did soccer." Uh, no, you didn't. So, how DO you study? Don't panic! It's okay if you don't know how: after all, there are no classes that teach it. But if you use these study hacks, you'll be ready and way less stressed about test day.

#1: Studying happens every day

You know how the night before your test you suddenly realize you don't know anything? You can totally avoid that feeling if you study a tiny bit EVERY DAY, not just the day before. Take five minutes each night to review what you've learned in class that day. You'll be way ahead in the game!

#2: Grill your teacher Your teacher is the one in charge of inventing your test, right? So, they know everything that's going to be on it. Now, they can't tell you exactly what the test questions will be, but it's totally fair for you to ask what topics you need to study.

#3: Make a study schedule They might sound lame, but study schedules make things TOTALLY easier to handle! So, how do you do it?

First, find out when your next test is.

Second, ask your teacher for a list of ALL of the topics on the test. if your test is on addition, your list might look like:

Things to study for the test I'm gonna ACE:
1. Adding positive and negative numbers
2. Addition facts
3. Column addition
4. Remembering to label place value

Third, get a calendar. If your school gave you an agenda, NOW is the time to use it, or you can make your own. Write down when you're going to study each of these things, so you can make sure you've left yourself enough time for everything before test day. Get a parent or friend to help you plan. Ta-da! Now you are on the way to totally acing your next test.

#4: Do questions It's easy to let yourself think that you know what's going on by flipping through your notes from class. But the best way to study is to do a TON of practice questions. Check your answers to make sure you're doing them right and go over anything that you have trouble with until you understand it. So, where can you find these practice questions?

1. Ask your teacher for extra questions that you can practise before your test. Get an answer sheet too.
2. Redo the homework questions that your teacher already gave you. Even if you've done them before, do them again!
3. Check online. Do a search for "worksheets" or "practice questions" and the topic.

#5: Know the lingo Sometimes the hardest part of a test is understanding what the question is asking you to do. Knowing your math words will help. Highlight all you can find in your homework and make a list. Make sure you know what each word means. Use the **memory hacks** so you don't forget them!

#6: Know your facts You're expected to know certain math facts from previous grades, even if they're not what the test is about. Like, your times tables from 1 to 10, even though you learned them a year ago. Once or twice a week, use an app or workbook for a refresh. Knowing the old stuff off by heart will help you answer test questions way faster.

#7: Test yourself Yes! Be the teacher and make yourself a practice test. Even more fun? Team up with a friend and pick different questions from your homework or that you did in class. Make up tests for each other, time it, and then take up the answers together.

#8: Study par-tay Order pizza, make some popcorn, and set yourself up at a big table with your friends. Study quietly for thirty minutes, and then take a fifteen-minute break to talk about your answers, or about anything you're stuck on. Get in a few good rounds of studying, then reward yourselves with a movie or dance off. Do it the weekend before your test and have a sleepover too!

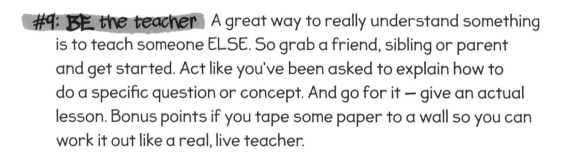

#9: BE the teacher A great way to really understand something is to teach someone ELSE. So grab a friend, sibling or parent and get started. Act like you've been asked to explain how to do a specific question or concept. And go for it — give an actual lesson. Bonus points if you tape some paper to a wall so you can work it out like a real, live teacher.

#10: Get those distractions OUTTA THERE Get away from anything that might distract you. Anything! The top reason that kids don't get the most out of their study time is distraction — a TV you can hear, a phone in your pocket or people nearby doing things. You need to make sure that you're somewhere you can concentrate.

#11: You do YOU Every single person is different — and only you know how you learn best! Do you need to study all alone or with people around? Do you need total silence or a bit of background music? The more tests you study for, the more you will get to know yourself. Take note of what works for you, and do things that way. Before you know it, you will become a boss-level math test study master!

HACK YOUR MARKS

Extra ways to help you boost your grade!

Marks matter, but they're not the ONLY thing. Some kids really struggle with tests, and that's okay! We all have strengths and weaknesses, and if tests aren't your best thing, you can work on that. For now, earn marks where you feel most comfortable. Assignments make up a huge part of your grade and you can usually do them with friends or at home, where you feel more chill. So, take the time to make sure that your assignments are complete and that you've done the best job possible, and hand them in ON TIME. You can always compare answers with a friend or have a parent look them over to make sure that everything is right as can be.

#1: Know where your marks come from Your grade comes from all sorts of places. Ask your teacher to explain where. Usually, participation, homework, assignments, quizzes and tests are all part of your overall grade. Maybe homework is worth more than you think and you're sometimes not so great about finishing it. Make a plan to change that! You have lots of chances to boost your marks every day.

#2: Go the extra mile If you're not feeling super great about your math mark, ask your teacher what you can do to make it better. Your teacher will have the answer, and then instead of just being all sad, you can actually DO SOMETHING about it!

#3: Raise your hand Many kids lose marks because they don't participate in class. Teachers LOVE to see that you're interested in what they're saying. Even if you don't know what's going on, raising your hand shows your teacher that you care. So hands up! Say something interesting, solve a problem at the board or ask a question — it all equals better marks.

#4: Ask your teacher for makeup work I know . . . no one wants MORE work. But putting in a bit of extra time is really going to help. If you don't do as great as you hoped on something, ask your teacher if you can redo it for extra marks. Or ask if you can do another test or worksheet or whatever instead. Sometimes they'll say yes, and that means higher marks for you.

#5: Spy on your class Is there a kid in your class who gets good marks? Find out how they do it! Ask them how they study for tests, do their homework or organize their binder. See if they want to study with you sometime. What works for them might not work for you, but it's seriously worth a try.

#6: Read your report card Your report card is full of info . . . about you! Sometimes the comments are confusing, so get your parents to set up a teacher interview. Go through the comments with your teacher and ask what you can do to improve.

HACK THE MATH!

NUMBERS

The Building Blocks of Math — and Your New BFFs!

What even IS a number? Sometimes even seeing a number can make you freak out, but you can just chill. Numbers help us count and describe all sorts of things. Numbers help us come up with cool ideas. Numbers are like the alphabet and we can use them to make the words and sentences of super-cool math stories.

Digits

Every number ever is made up of one or more digits! Just think of digits as the ABCs of the math world. The English alphabet has twenty-six letters, and the math alphabet has ten digits! After all, math is just a language — and once you learn to speak it, OMG! When you become BFFs with math, you can do anything.

The ten digits are:
0 1 2 3 4 5 6 7 8 9

WAIT! Why is 10 not a digit? Look closely: 10 is simply 1 and 0 stuck next to one another. It's a NUMBER made up of TWO digits, or what we call a two-digit number! Notice that all of the digits are less than 10. They're what we call "ones" because they're made up of one digit! Once you've got the digits down, you are ready to tackle the magical world of math.

43

Place Value

What does that mean? When we look at numbers with more than a single digit, we've got to figure out what each of the digits in that number mean. **Place value** literally means "how much is this digit in this spot worth?" Don't worry, here's how to figure that out. Let's get started and meet a ginormous number!

Meet $5,892,643$!

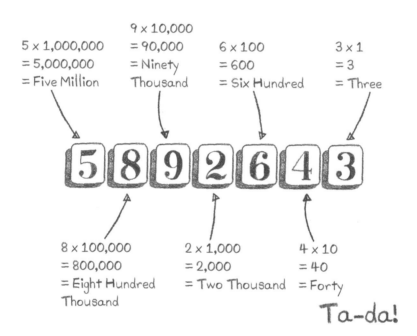

5 x 1,000,000
= 5,000,000
= Five Million

9 x 10,000
= 90,000
= Ninety Thousand

6 x 100
= 600
= Six Hundred

3 x 1
= 3
= Three

8 x 100,000
= 800,000
= Eight Hundred Thousand

2 x 1,000
= 2,000
= Two Thousand

4 x 10
= 40
= Forty

Ta-da!

Say It Out Loud!

Want to sound like a total pro when reading big numbers out loud? Use these two hacks:

1. NEVER use the word "and" when reading a number! We need to save that word for decimals, which we'll get to later.

2. Moving from RIGHT to LEFT, there is a comma every three digits, and each one has a name. The first one is "thousand." Move three spots to the left of thousand, and that comma's name is "million." And if your number is super ginormous, three MORE spots to the left of million would be "billion!"

3. How does that work? Check it out:

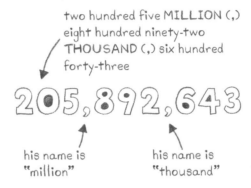

two hundred five MILLION (,)
eight hundred ninety-two
THOUSAND (,) six hundred
forty-three

205,892,643

his name is
"million"

his name is
"thousand"

So you'd say "two hundred five million (,) eight hundred ninety-two thousand (,) six hundred forty-three!"

Comparing Numbers

To compare small numbers, the easiest thing to do is use a number line — more on that on page 52. When we have BIG numbers, though, we like to line things up nice and neat so that we can see what's going on. How can you tell which number is the biggest? Comparing numbers is super easy. Take a look!

Q: Which of the following numbers is the biggest?
(3,581)   3,467   2,089

45

Step 1: Line up the numbers on top of each other, making sure that every digit is in the right place-value position.

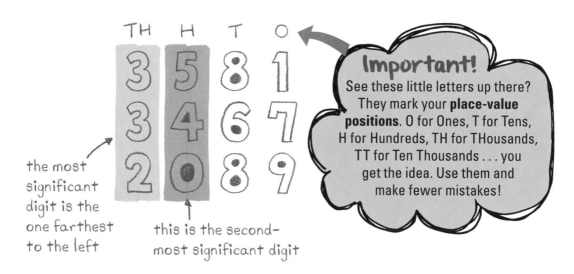

TH   H   T   O

3 5 8 1
3 4 6 7
2 0 8 9

the most significant digit is the one farthest to the left

this is the second-most significant digit

Important!
See these little letters up there? They mark your **place-value positions**. O for Ones, T for Tens, H for Hundreds, TH for THousands, TT for Ten Thousands . . . you get the idea. Use them and make fewer mistakes!

Step 2: The digit farthest to the left is the most important — or significant! Since the top two numbers have matching 3s, they're tied for first place. The bottom guy is out — it only has a **significant digit** of 2! Now, with only those top two numbers in the running, we move right, to our second-most significant digit! We can see that 5 is bigger than 4, which means that our top number — 3,581 — is THE BIGGEST!

A: **3,581 is the biggest number.**

A **significant digit** is just like what it sounds like: the most important one! These guys are in the place-value position worth the most. So, when you read the number from left to right, the leftmost number is the most significant, the one to the right of that the second-most significant, the one to the right of THAT the third-most significant and so on!

Rounding Numbers

Rounding just means changing a number to another number that's easier to remember but that's pretty close to its original value. There are two ways we can round: down or up.

Rounding DOWN: If your digit is 4 or less, turn it into a zero but DO NOT add 1 to the digit to its left — just leave it alone!

Rounding UP: If your digit is 5 or more, turn that sucker into a big fat zero and add 1 to the digit to the left of it.

Step 1: Figure out which place value we want to round to. Look at what your question is asking. If it's rounding to tens, it means finding what ten or multiple of ten it is closest too — like, 0, 10, 20, 30, 40, 50, 60, 70, 80, 90, or 100 and everything to the right flips to zero. If it's rounding to hundreds, it would be 0, 100, 200, 300 … you get the drill, right?

Step 2: Start with the digit to the RIGHT of that place value and start a-roundin'! Let's see it in action:

Q: Round 7,842 to the nearest ten!

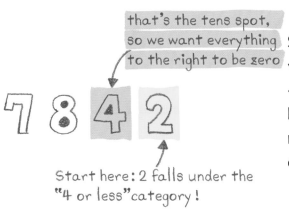

that's the tens spot, so we want everything to the right to be zero

Start here: 2 falls under the "4 or less" category!

Step 1: Figure out what place value we want to round to — the tens spot! Highlight it! Now look at the digit to the right. It's a 2, so we're using our **"round down"** rule.

Step 2: We turn that 2 into a zero, and then the 4 in the tens spot stays how it is.

A: **Rounding 7,842 to the nearest ten gives us 7,840.**

Let's try another one:

Q: **Round 7,846 to the nearest ten.**

Step 1: Figure out what place value we want to round to — the tens spot! Highlight it. Now look at the digit to the right. It's a 6, so we're using our **"round up"** rule.

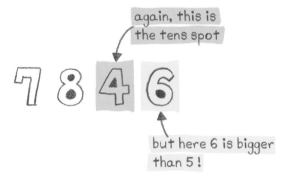

again, this is the tens spot

but here 6 is bigger than 5 !

Step 2: We turn that 6 into a zero, and then add 1 to the 4 in the tens spot, which makes it 5! Simple, right?

A: **7,846 rounded to the nearest ten is 7,850.**

48

Let's try ONE more!

Q: Round 7,846 to the nearest hundred — you can do it! *7800*

Okay, so this might seem a BIT trickier but no worries — it's all about finding the right place value to start with.

Step 1: So, what place value do we want to round to? Right, the hundreds spot! Highlight it! Remember, you're turning everything to the RIGHT of the 8 into big, round ZEROS!

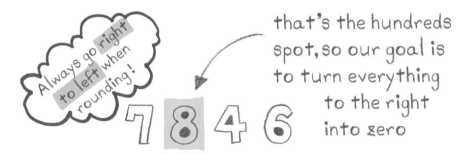

Always go right to left when rounding!

that's the hundreds spot, so our goal is to turn everything to the right into zero

Step 2: Take a look at the number to the right of that 8. It's the next significant digit and it's a 4. That's less than 5 so we round down.

Start here! 4 is "5 or less" so we round down

Step 3: The tens spot decided it! Everything to the right of the 8 changes to nice, round zeros … and you're done!

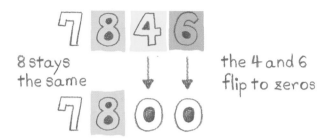

8 stays the same

the 4 and 6 flip to zeros

A: **7,846 rounded to the nearest hundred is 7,800!**

BONUS ROUND! **Q: Round 7,856 to the nearest hundred!** 7900

Step 1: It's all about the tens spot again. This time, we've got a 5 so we're rounding up. Rounding up pushes the 8 up to 9, and everything to the right of the hundreds spot flips to a zero.

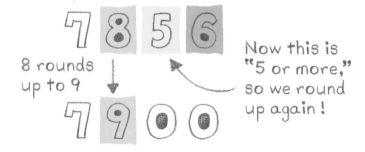

8 rounds up to 9

Now this is "5 or more," so we round up again!

A: **7,856 rounded to the nearest hundred is 7,900!**

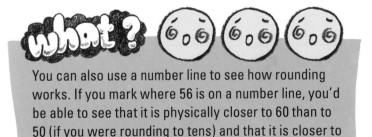

what?

You can also use a number line to see how rounding works. If you mark where 56 is on a number line, you'd be able to see that it is physically closer to 60 than to 50 (if you were rounding to tens) and that it is closer to 100 than to zero (if you were rounding to hundreds).

Repeat and remember!

To round a digit, look next door: 5 or higher, add one more; 4 or lower, just ignore!

Rounding to Significant Digits

Sometimes you might be asked to round to significant digits (a.k.a. "sig digits") — no biggie! First, how many sig digits do they want you to round to? Find out! Once you know, your goal is to turn all your digits to the right of that into zeros! Remember, the MOST sig digit is the farthest left, and then as we move to the right, digits become less and less significant. There are three different ways to round 7,846, depending on how many sig digits are asked for!

Whole Numbers

Before we get any deeper into numbers, you need to know that the basic kind is a **whole number**. That's a number that doesn't include any tiny part of a number less than one. So, like, no fraction or decimal part. Some awesome examples of whole numbers are 1, 42 and 1,234,567,890. And negative numbers are NOT ALLOWED. Wait, what's a negative number? Turn the page to find out . . .

Number Lines

Number lines are a super-cool way to see how positive and negative numbers work. They're also really useful for adding and subtracting. Here's how one works:

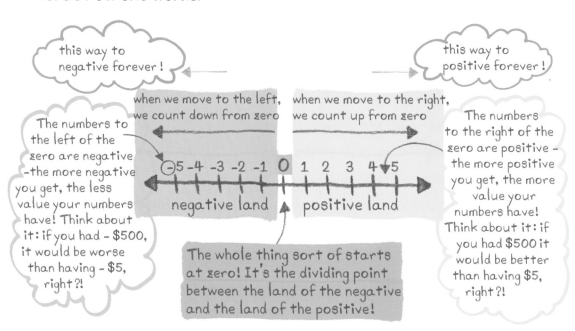

this way to negative forever!

this way to positive forever!

when we move to the left, we count down from zero

when we move to the right, we count up from zero

The numbers to the left of the zero are negative —the more negative you get, the less value your numbers have! Think about it: if you had - $500, it would be worse than having - $5, right?!

The numbers to the right of the zero are positive — the more positive you get, the more value your numbers have! Think about it: if you had $500 it would be better than having $5, right?!

-5 -4 -3 -2 -1 0 1 2 3 4 5

negative land   positive land

The whole thing sort of starts at zero! It's the dividing point between the land of the negative and the land of the positive!

Feeling stuck? Think of it this way!

Because we read from left to right, we look at number lines the same way! When we're moving from left to right, we call it "counting up," because it seems more natural — just like with reading! When we're moving from right to left, we call it "counting down."

Get to Know Positive and Negative Numbers

Positive numbers are the ones you're probably used to. They're the numbers greater than zero. Now, let's take a look at negative numbers, which are actually really useful and kind of cool!

Negative Numbers

What even are they? Okay, deep breaths: just like there is sweet and salty in this world, there are ALSO positive AND negative numbers! That might seem crazy, but soon you'll see that it totally makes sense and that we need them both! A negative number is just a number that's LESS than zero. Look! Here's one now: -3. You might also see this "negative three" guy written like this: (-3). Not so scary, right?

Sometimes in calculations we put negative numbers in brackets so that they are easier to read and we don't confuse the negative symbol with a minus sign because they look the same. So, you might see your negative numbers written either like this: -5, or like this: (-5). Don't worry, they're the same thing!

Fancy lingo!
Want to sound super smart? **Integers** is the word for all positive and negative whole numbers.

Doing Actual Math with Positive and Negative Numbers

No problem! If you know how to add and subtract regular numbers . . . you'll be all set to do it with negative numbers too. It's easy to see how it all works using a number line. Just follow the instructions and it will become totally natural. Soon you'll be like, "I got this!"

Adding two positive numbers

Q: Use a number line to work out 1 + 3.

No biggie! Just mark your starting point, which is 1. Now move to the RIGHT on the number line by whatever you're adding. Here we're adding 3, so we move 3 steps from 1 on the number line to get 4!

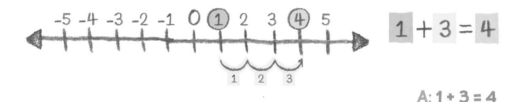

$$1 + 3 = 4$$

A: 1 + 3 = 4

Adding a positive and a negative number

When you add a negative number, it's really a subtraction question in disguise, so we move LEFT on the number line.

Q: Now let's try 1 + (–3) = ?! (– 2)

You've got this! Just mark your starting point, which is 1. Now move to the LEFT on the number line by whatever you're adding. Here, we're adding -3, so we move 3 steps to the left of 1 to get to -2!

$$1 + (- 3) = - 2$$

A: 1 + (-3) = -2

Subtracting a positive number

When we subtract, we move LEFT on the number line. And if we go all the way to the left of zero into negativeland, that's okay!

Q: 1 - 3 = ? (~2)

Mark your starting point, which is 1. Now, because we're subtracting, we move 3 steps to the LEFT on the number line to get to -2!

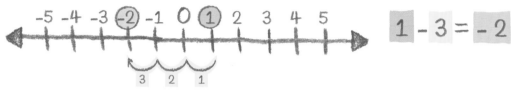

$$1 - 3 = -2$$

A: 1 - 3 = -2

Subtracting a negative number

Ready for this? When you subtract a negative number, you are really just ADDING — the minus signs cancel each other out. Super easy!

Q: 1 - (-3) = ?

Just mark your starting point, which is 1. Now move 3 steps to the RIGHT on the number line to get to 4!

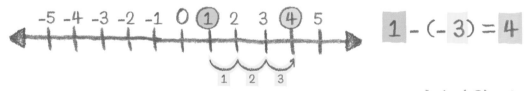

$$1 - (-3) = 4$$

A: 1 - (-3) = 4

Your starting point is always the **first number** in your question and then you move left or right. Do NOT start at zero! So, if your question is 5 + 3, that means you START at 5, and then move to the right from there.

Pro Tip!

Here's a hack that I like to use with positive and negative numbers. Using this trick, we only have to remember TWO tips:

If two signs are next to each other and the SAME, we're adding
(going TO THE RIGHT on the number line)

$1 + 3$ is the same as $1 + {+}3$ remember, if there's no sign, it's positive! This is just normal addition, no funny business! $= 4$

$1 - (-3)$ is the same as $1 - (-3)$ the two signs are the same, so we can mush them into one big addition sign $= 4$

If two signs are next to each other and DIFFERENT, we're subtracting
(going TO THE LEFT on the number line)

$1 - 3$ is the same as $1 - {+}3 = -2$

$1 + (-3)$ is the same as $1 + {-}3 = -2$

$(-1) + (-3)$ is the same as $-(1 + 3) = -4$

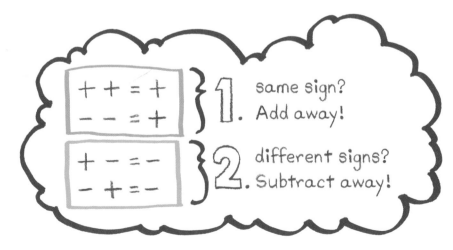

$+ \; + \; = \; +$
$- \; - \; = \; +$
1. same sign? Add away!

$+ \; - \; = \; -$
$- \; + \; = \; -$
2. different signs? Subtract away!

ADDITION

Math + Hacks = Fun!

What even is it? When we bring two or more amounts together to make a bigger amount, we call that addition! There are two cool ways of thinking about adding: as **totalling** and as **increasing**. Use whichever works for you — they're both the same thing in the end.

Watch out for these keywords! If you see these magic words, they're probably talking about addition:

COUNT ON
SUM TOTAL
go up by PLUS More
Increase By
Altogether

Fancy lingo!
The answer of an addition question is the **sum** or the **total**.

Addition as Totalling

When we think of addition as totalling, we think of it as mushing two amounts together to make a whole new amount. We call this new amount the **sum**.

Let's say you have 5 pink gumballs and your BFF has 3 blue gumballs. If you pour all the gumballs into one big pile and count them, you'll have a TOTAL of 8 gumballs. So, the **sum** of 5 and 3 is 8, or we can write this as 5 + 3 = 8!

8 is the sum of 5 and 3

$$5 + 3 = 8$$

Order doesn't matter for addition! Seriously, the order the numbers are in doesn't matter! When it comes to addition, 3 + 5 is the same as 5 + 3. They both equal 8. The fancy name for this rule is the **commutative property**.

Addition as Increasing

When we think of addition as increasing, we think of increasing some original amount by a specific quantity, and then figuring out what the new amount is by counting UP from the original!

Say you have 5 pink gumballs and your friend gives you 3 blue gumballs (because that's what friends are for, right?). To figure out how many gumballs you now have, you just count up (hint: to the right) from the amount of gumballs you started with. The easiest way to do this is with a number line.

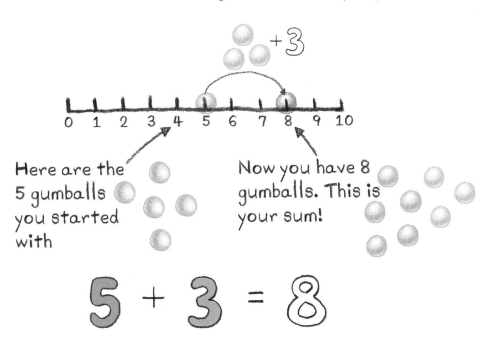

Here we're increasing your original amount by 3 gumballs

+3

Here are the 5 gumballs you started with

Now you have 8 gumballs. This is your sum!

5 + 3 = 8

The Real Deal: Column Addition

When we're dealing with smaller numbers, it's easy to use a number line to add. But when we have bigger numbers, it's time to break out our secret weapon: column addition! You can use this method to add ANY numbers together, even ones with decimals. Here's how it's done:

Q: 396 + 257 = ?

Step 1: Start by writing one number on top of the other. Pay attention to place value! It is totally important that digits with the same place value are directly on top of each another. Remember, it doesn't matter which number goes on the top or bottom because, hey, the **commutative property**!

Step 2: Now we're going to add each of the digits in the top row to the digit underneath it in the bottom row, starting on the far right with the ones column. We're going to do one column at a time.

Cool Trick!
Try labelling your place value columns with H / T / O. You don't have to, but it helps!

60

Step ③

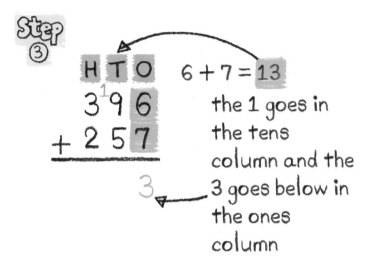

H T O

6 + 7 = 13

the 1 goes in the tens column and the 3 goes below in the ones column

Step 3: Add 6 to 7 and you get 13. Now write the 3 in the ones column. That's it! The 1 stands for 1 ten, so we're going to carry it over to the tens column by writing a teeny "1" near the top. This will help us remember to add it in when we get to the tens column in the next step.

Step ④

this 1 is carried over from our calculation that we JUST did in the tens column

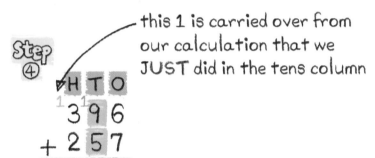

9 + 5 = 14 BUT remember we have that extra 1 that we carried over from step 3 14 + 1 = 15.

Step 4: Since the ones are done, we move left, over to the tens column. Again, add down, so add 9 tens to 5 tens and you get 14 tens. But remember — you have the 1 ten that we carried over from the ones, so add that to 14 and you get 15 tens! Write the 5 below the line in the tens column, and carry over the 1 to the hundreds column.

Feeling stuck? Think of it this way!

When we carry that 1 from the 15 over to the hundreds column, remember that we're saying, "Hey, we have TEN extra tens here!" That's why the 1 gets moved over to the hundreds column — because ten tens is the same as 10 x 10, which equals 100.

61

Step 5: What now? You guessed it! Add the hundreds column the exact same way you added the other columns. So, 3 hundreds plus 2 hundreds gives us 5 hundreds, then throw in that 1 you carried over and you've got 6 hundreds. Write that below the line in the hundreds column and you are done.

A: 396 + 257 = 653

$3 + 2 + 1 = 6$

Pro Tips for Addition!

#1: No decimal drama Got some decimals to deal with? We add numbers with decimals using column addition the EXACT same way we add normal numbers. Check out the Decimals section for an example.

#2: Multiple numbers Using column addition, you can add up as many numbers as you want, and those numbers can have any number of digits. Just be careful when lining them up on top of each other. Make sure that each digit gets entered in the right place-value column. For example, 1,034 + 25 + 7 would look like this:

#3: Carry over amounts

Sometimes when you're adding a bunch of numbers, you may end up with a bigger amount to carry over, like 20 or 70 or more. Just carry the 2 or the 7 (or whatever) like so:

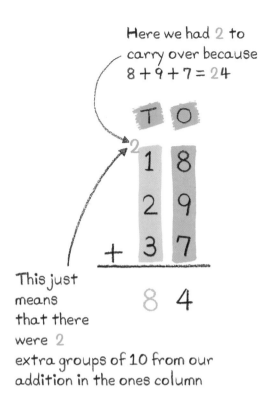

Here we had 2 to carry over because $8 + 9 + 7 = 24$

This just means that there were 2 extra groups of 10 from our addition in the ones column

#4: Blank spaces are okay!

If you're adding digits and find that there's nothing beneath them in the column, don't freak. You're basically adding zero, because there's nothing there! Just add the numbers in the column and ignore the blank spaces:

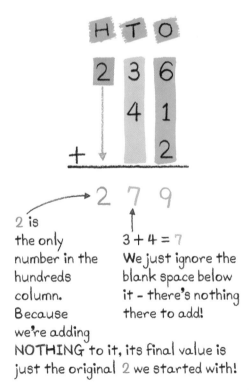

2 is the only number in the hundreds column. Because we're adding NOTHING to it, its final value is just the original 2 we started with!

$3 + 4 = 7$ We just ignore the blank space below it - there's nothing there to add!

SUBTRACTION

Less Is More Fun!

What even is it? Subtraction is just the opposite of addition! Instead of bringing amounts together to make more, we're taking an amount away from another amount to get less. There are two ways of looking at subtraction: you can think of it as taking away, or you can think of it as finding the difference between two numbers.

Watch out for these keywords! If you see them in a word problem, they're probably talking about subtraction.

decrease by
REDUCE REMOVE
TAKE AWAY SUBTRACT
how many left?
Less Go Down By
Than go back by

Subtraction as Finding the Difference

One way we can think of subtraction is as finding the difference between two amounts. When we do it this way, we're comparing quantities, but not actually taking anything away. We're basically saying, "Hey, how many steps would it take to get from this one number to another bigger number?" That answer is called the **difference** and it's the same answer we would get if we subtracted the smaller number from the bigger number.

You can try this on a number line. You have 5 pink gumballs and your friend has 3 blue gumballs. To find out the difference between your two piles of gumballs, start at the smaller number and figure out how many steps or jumps it takes to get to the bigger number!

We can see that the difference between the two piles of gumballs is 2, which is the same thing as saying 5 - 3 = 2

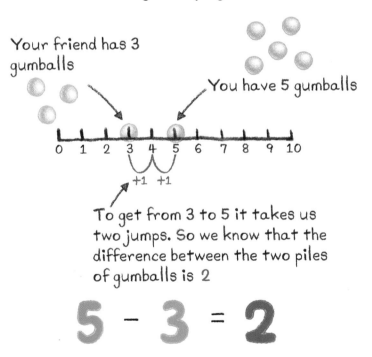

Your friend has 3 gumballs

You have 5 gumballs

0 1 2 3 4 5 6 7 8 9 10

+1 +1

To get from 3 to 5 it takes us two jumps. So we know that the difference between the two piles of gumballs is 2

5 − 3 = 2

Subtraction as Taking Away

Another easy way to look at subtraction with positive numbers is simply to see it as the opposite of addition. On a number line, that means we move to the left instead of to the right.

Let's say you have 5 pink gumballs and — because you're the best friend ever! — you decide to give your friend 3 of them. To figure out how many gumballs you have leftover, you just count down (hint: to the left) from the original amount of gumballs you started with. The easiest way to do this is with a number line.

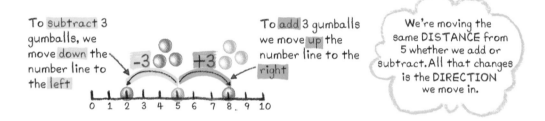

To subtract 3 gumballs, we move down the number line to the left

To add 3 gumballs we move up the number line to the right

We're moving the same DISTANCE from 5 whether we add or subtract. All that changes is the DIRECTION we move in.

After taking away 3 gumballs from your stash to give to your friend, you have 2 gumballs left. Proving that you are also super nice.

Order TOTALLY matters for subtraction! This is IMPORTANT! When you're adding numbers together, it doesn't matter what order you add them in. BUT when you are subtracting, it does matter. For example, is 10 – 1 the same as 1 – 10? Nope! Even without actually calculating it, you know that those are two very different things. You MUST perform subtraction in the order that the numbers appear in.

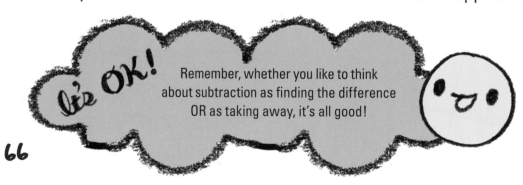

It's OK!

Remember, whether you like to think about subtraction as finding the difference OR as taking away, it's all good!

The Real Deal: Column Subtraction

When you're dealing with smaller numbers, you can totally just use a number line to subtract. We talked about this in the Numbers chapter, so head over there to remind yourself of how simple number lines can be. But when we have bigger numbers, it's time to break out our secret weapon: column subtraction!

Remember how column addition was, like, the best thing ever? Well, column subtraction is pretty much the same — it allows us to subtract ANY two numbers. Don't stress about carrying stuff over — just remember that those friendly numbers to the left of the digits we're subtracting are happy to let us borrow from them. Ready to rock?

Q: 832 - 675 = ?

Step 1: Write the number you're subtracting **from** (832) on the top, and the number that you're taking away from it (675) on the bottom. Hint: the number with the higher value usually goes on top, and the number with the lesser value below it, but check the question to be sure: in this case, the first number goes on top. Pay attention to place value — it's important that digits with the same place value are directly on top of one another.

Seriously, LABEL YOUR PLACE-VALUE COLUMNS! It's so easy to make mistakes when you don't.

Step 2: Now we're going to subtract each of the digits in the bottom row from the digit above it in the top row, starting with the ones column on the right. Do ONE column at a time.

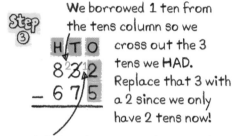

We borrowed 1 ten from the tens column so we cross out the 3 tens we HAD. Replace that 3 with a 2 since we only have 2 tens now!

We bring the 1 ten we borrowed over to the ones column. We turned it into 10 ones so now we have 12 instead of 2 because $10 + 2 = 12$

Step 3: Wait, what?! How can we subtract that big 5 from that tiny 2? By borrowing from our tens neighbour, of course! There are 3 tens just chilling there, so grab 1 ten and turn it into 10 ones. Remember to SHOW we did this by writing a 1 in the ones column and turning our 3 in the tens column into a 2.

Step 4: Now subtract 5 ones from the 12 ones we have in that ones column! $12 - 5 = 7$, so put that 7 under the answer line, in the ones column.

Feeling stuck? Think of it this way!

When you borrow a ten from the tens column, you're EXCHANGING that 1 ten for 10 ones. They're just different ways of representing the same thing. That's why you're allowed to put that new 1 in the ones column, turning the 2 into a 12. You're actually ADDING 10 to the 2.

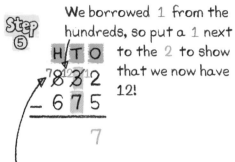

Step ⑤

We borrowed 1 from the hundreds, so put a 1 next to the 2 to show that we now have 12!

Change 8 to 7 to show that we borrowed 1 of those hundreds!

Step 5: The ones are done, so we move left to the tens column. Again, subtract the bottom from the top, so 7 from 2 . . . but OMG, same problem! So, we borrow from our neighbour to the left again. Just exchange 1 of the hundreds for 10 tens. Write a 1 next to the 2 to show that you have 12 tens. Now change the 8 in the hundreds column to a 7 to show that we exchanged 1 of those hundreds for 10 tens.

Step ⑥

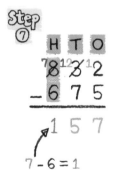

12 - 7 = 5

Step 6: Go ahead and subtract 7 tens from 12 tens.

Step ⑦

H	T	O
7 8	12 3	1 2
− 6	7	5

1 5 7

7 - 6 = 1

Step 7: Final step! Move left to the hundreds column. No problems here — just subtract 6 from 7, to get 1.

A: 832 − 675 = 157

69

Pro Tips for Subtraction!

Here are some of the places where it's easy to get confused:

#1 Decimal drama? No way! You subtract numbers with decimals the EXACT same way — more on that in the Decimals chapter.

#2 Different number of digits? All you need to do is make sure that each digit gets entered in the right place-value column, so be careful when stacking them. For example 1,032 – 21 would look like this:

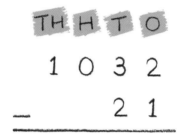

$$
\begin{array}{cccc}
\text{TH} & \text{H} & \text{T} & \text{O} \\
1 & 0 & 3 & 2 \\
- & & 2 & 1 \\
\hline
\end{array}
$$

#3: No number? If you're subtracting and find that there isn't a number beneath one of the digits in a column, don't worry! It's like you're just subtracting zero, because there's nothing there.

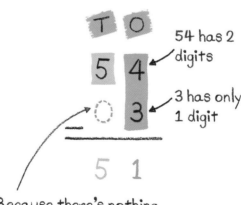

54 has 2 digits

3 has only 1 digit

Because there's nothing there, we think of it as a zero. 5 – 0 = 5

MULTIPLICATION!

It's Ten Times the Fun!

Multiplication seems like this big, bad, scary monster. But not only is multiplication about as scary as a kitten, it's fun! There are so many cool little tricks you can use. It takes work and practice — but hey, most of the amazing things in life DO.

What even is it? There are a bunch of ways to talk about multiplication, but they all just mean the same thing. I like to think of it as adding together lots of quantities of the SAME size, or to think of it as scaling.

Watch out for these keywords! If you see them, they're probably talking about multiplication.

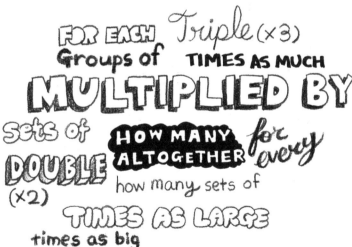

FOR EACH
Triple (×3)
Groups of   TIMES AS MUCH
MULTIPLIED BY
sets of   HOW MANY ALTOGETHER   for every
DOUBLE (×2)
how many sets of
TIMES AS LARGE
times as big

X marks the spot!

"x" is the symbol we use to multiply numbers together. So, 3 x 2 means 3 multiplied by 2. Another way of saying this is **"3 times 2"**!

Know the lingo! There are all sorts of important words we use when talking about multiplication, so let's run through those first.

Factor: Factors are the numbers we multiply together to get another number.

Product: The number we get when we multiply factors together is called a product. This is usually the answer of a multiplication question.

Multiple: When we multiply factors together, we can also use the word "multiple" to describe the answer we get — but it has a special role.

Let's do an example with these cool words!

$$3 \times 2 = 6$$

3 and 2 are factors of 6
6 is the product of 3 times 2
6 is a multiple of 3
6 is also a multiple of 2

Now we can also take that 6, which we got as our answer in the first example, and multiply it by ANY number. The result will be a multiple of 6!

$$6 \times 2 = 12$$
$$6 \times 3 = 18$$
$$6 \times 4 = 24$$

12, 18 and 24 are ALL multiples of 6!

Order doesn't matter! Multiplication is like addition when it comes to order — it doesn't matter! Remember that fancy name for this rule? The **commutative property**! So, 3 x 4 is the same as 4 x 3 ... they both equal 12!

72

Two Ways of Thinking about Multiplication!

Multiplication as Repeated Addition

Multiplication is a super-useful tool to use when you have groups of the same size that need to be added together a bunch of times.

Let's say you're looking at the night sky and notice a patch of 5 stars. Then you look a bit closer and realize that you see 3 patches of 5 stars in the sky. You want to know how many stars you see in total, but you don't want to add every single star — that would take too long! So, we multiply! What we're actually doing is adding 5 to ITSELF 3 times — and that's what multiplication is. It's adding a number to itself a certain number of times. So, all we have to do is multiply 3 by 5 to find out that we have 15 stars!

If you're ever in a crunch and all of your multiplication tricks have left your brain, first take a breath and chill. Remember that multiplication is just repeated addition, and it will be okay!

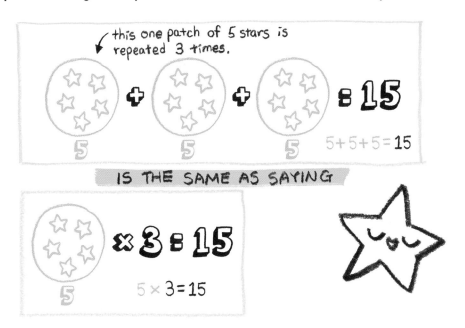

this one patch of 5 stars is repeated 3 times.

$5 + 5 + 5 = 15$

IS THE SAME AS SAYING

$5 \times 3 = 15$

Multiplication as Scaling

Another way to think of multiplication is changing the size of an object, which we call **scaling**. This is super useful because that's what we're doing when we multiply with fractions.

Yes, multiplying with fractions is a thing. But don't freak out — more on that on page 132! And it can be tricky to totally understand it because when we think of multiplying, we usually think of making things bigger. BUT things are different when fractions are involved. Just remember that multiplying with proper fractions (fractions that are less than 1) always makes the product smaller than the factors — not bigger!

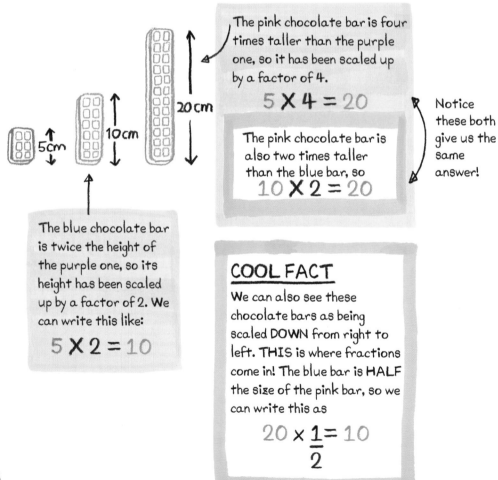

The pink chocolate bar is four times taller than the purple one, so it has been scaled up by a factor of 4.

$$5 \times 4 = 20$$

The pink chocolate bar is also two times taller than the blue bar, so

$$10 \times 2 = 20$$

Notice these both give us the same answer!

The blue chocolate bar is twice the height of the purple one, so its height has been scaled up by a factor of 2. We can write this like:

$$5 \times 2 = 10$$

COOL FACT

We can also see these chocolate bars as being scaled DOWN from right to left. THIS is where fractions come in! The blue bar is HALF the size of the pink bar, so we can write this as

$$20 \times \frac{1}{2} = 10$$

Times Tables — Your Secret Weapon to Math Superstardom!

Here's something super important. Like, the most important thing EVER. Literally EVERYONE complains about doing their times tables. It's a thing. But not knowing your tables can have a serious impact later. When you get to high school math, you're going to be doing super-cool stuff — but to do it like a boss, you gotta know them! Here's a secret: memorizing the times tables is not actually hard. The trick is that you have to just, like, get INTO it. And here are ways to do exactly that.

Pro Tips!

I have two fave ways of memorizing times tables:

#1 Flash cards I LOVE making multiplication flash cards! Equation on one side, answer on the other. You can make them cool (Pokémon! Puppies!), but JUST DO IT and use them to practise.

#2 Write them down Seriously — over and over again. Like, one day just write the 2 times table five times in a row. The next day, do the 3s. Then the day after that, do the 2s again to make sure you remember. And keep going until you've done ALL of them! It might take a few weeks, but get this: then you will know them and you'll be set for math all the way to high school!

The Grid!

The multiplication grid is a handy way to arrange all of the times tables in one place. It might look overwhelming, but it's really easy to use and a great way to get to know them!

The **factors** appear along the top and the left side of the grid. The **products** of those factors are in the middle of the grid!

×	1	2	3	4	5	6	7	8	9	10	11	12
1	1	2	3	4	5	6	7	8	9	10	11	12
2	2	4	6	8	10	12	14	16	18	20	22	24
3	3	6	9	12	15	18	21	24	27	30	33	36
4	4	8	12	16	20	24	28	32	36	40	44	48
5	5	10	15	20	25	30	35	40	45	50	55	60
6	6	12	18	24	30	36	42	48	54	60	66	72
7	7	14	21	28	35	42	49	56	63	70	77	84
8	8	16	24	32	40	48	56	64	72	80	88	96
9	9	18	27	36	45	54	63	72	81	90	99	108
10	10	20	30	40	50	60	70	80	90	100	110	120
11	11	22	33	44	55	66	77	88	99	110	121	132
12	12	24	36	48	60	72	84	96	108	120	132	144

Let me show you how to use this handy-dandy grid by finding 4 x 6.

Q: **4 x 6 = ?**

Step ① First let's find the first factor on top of the grid. Our first factor is 4!

Step ② Now we need to find our second factor, 6, along the left side of the grid!

Step ③ Now find the spot where both of those factors meet! That spot is 24!

×	1	2	3	4	5	6	7	8	9	10	11	12
1	1	2	3	4	5	6	7	8	9	10	11	12
2	2	4	6	8	10	12	14	16	18	20	22	24
3	3	6	9	12	15	18	21	24	27	30	33	36
4	4	8	12	16	20	24	28	32	36	40	44	48
5	5	10	15	20	25	30	35	40	45	50	55	60
6	6	12	18	24	30	36	42	48	54	60	66	72
7	7	14	21	28	35	42	49	56	63	70	77	84
8	8	16	24	32	40	48	56	64	72	80	88	96
9	9	18	27	36	45	54	63	72	81	90	99	108
10	10	20	30	40	50	60	70	80	90	100	110	120
11	11	22	33	44	55	66	77	88	99	110	121	132
12	12	24	36	48	60	72	84	96	108	120	132	144

A: **4 x 6 = 24**

Remember how I said that multiplication can be done in any order? That means you could have found the 6 on the top part of the grid and the 4 along the left if you wanted to. Either way works!

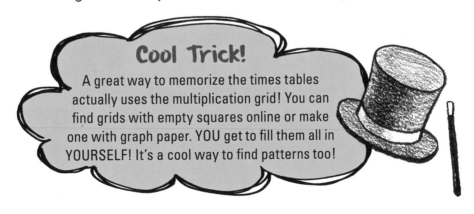

Cool Trick!

A great way to memorize the times tables actually uses the multiplication grid! You can find grids with empty squares online or make one with graph paper. YOU get to fill them all in YOURSELF! It's a cool way to find patterns too!

Impress Your Friends with Mental Multiplication Magic

Honestly, memorizing your times tables is, like, the BEST math thing you can do for yourself, ever. It's also fun to use multiplication tricks to remember some of them. Your friends will be like, "OMG, how did you do that in your head?!"

Multiplying by 2 Just double the number — so, add it to itself!

$$2 \times 9 = ?$$

$$9 + 9 = 18$$

just add the number to itself!

Multiplying by 3 Map it out on a tic-tac-toe grid!

$1 \times 3 = 3$	$2 \times 3 = 6$	$3 \times 3 = 9$
03	06	09
$4 \times 3 = 12$	$5 \times 3 = 15$	$6 \times 3 = 18$
12	15	18
$7 \times 3 = 21$	$8 \times 3 = 24$	$9 \times 3 = 27$
21	24	27

Step 1: Draw a tic-tac-toe grid.

Step 2: Count up from 1, starting at the lower left corner.

Step 3: Number the left digit across rows starting at zero.

Multiplying by 4 Since multiplying by 2 is doubling, multiplying by 4 is doubling twice.

$$4 \times 9 = ?$$

$$2 \times 9 = 18$$ First, just double the number

$$2 \times 18 = 36$$ Now, double it again!

$$4 \times 9 = 36$$

Multiplying by 5: even numbers If you're multiplying an **even** number by 5, divide the number by 2, then tack a zero on the end!

$$6 \times 5 = ?$$

$$6 \div 2 = 3$$ divide the number by 2

$$6 \times 5 = 30$$ stick a 0 on the end

Multiplying by 5: odd numbers If you're multiplying an **odd** number by 5, subtract 1 from your number, THEN divide by 2, THEN tack a 5 on the end!

$$7 \times 5 = ?$$

$$7 - 1 = 6$$ Subtract 1 from the number

$$6 \div 2 = 3$$ Divide the result by 2

Stick a 5 on the end

$$7 \times 5 = 35$$

Multiplying by 6 When you multiply an even number by 6, your answer ends in the same digit as that number!

$$6 \times 2 = 12 - \text{They both end in 2!}$$
$$6 \times 4 = 24 - \text{They both end in 4!}$$
$$6 \times 8 = 48 - \text{They both end in 8!}$$

Multiplying by 7 Okay, this is a crazy one that hardly anyone knows! Make a grid like the one below. Working across each row gives you the final digit of what you get when you multiply by 7, starting with 1.

First, write out the digits from 1 to 9, like this!

Second, look at the times table and match up the digits in the chart!

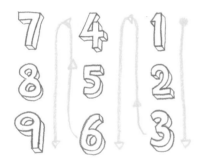

This gives the final digit of each item in the table in order.

$1 \times 7 = 7$ $2 \times 7 = 14$ $3 \times 7 = 21$
$4 \times 7 = 28$ $5 \times 7 = 35$ $6 \times 7 = 42$
$7 \times 7 = 49$ $8 \times 7 = 56$ $9 \times 7 = 63$
$10 \times 7 = 70$ $11 \times 7 = 77$ $12 \times 7 = 84$

Cool Trick!
$56 = 7 \times 8$ Get it?
Because: 5, 6, 7, 8!

Multiplying by 8 Repeat after me: "Double once, double twice, double THRICE (which means three times)!" That's how we multiply by 8! Let's try it with 3 x 8:

Double once: $3 \times 2 = 6$
Double twice: $6 \times 2 = 12$
Double thrice: $12 \times 2 = 24$
$3 \times 8 = 24$

Got it? Let's try it with 7, so 7 x 8.

Double once: 7 × 2 = 14
Double twice: 14 × 2 = 28
Double thrice: 28 × 2 = 56
7 × 8 = 56

Multiplying by 9 For the first digit of the product, subtract 1 from the factor you are multiplying by 9. The second digit of the product is 9 minus the first digit. Like this!

$$9 \times 4 = ?$$

$$4 - 1 = 3$$

$$9 - 3 = 6$$

$$9 \times 4 = 36$$

Multiplying by 10 Multiplying by 10 is so easy that it's almost a joke! All you have to do is throw a zero on the end! You're done . . . and ready to party!

10 × 3 = ?
10 × 3 = 30 – Just add a zero and you're done!

Multiplying by 11 If you're multiplying 11 by any number from 1 to 9, all you have to do is write the digit you're multiplying twice.

$$8 \times 11 = 88$$

If you're multiplying any 2-digit number by 11, we've got you covered! Write the digits with a space in between. Then add the digits together and plop their sum in the space!

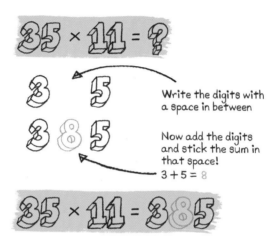

Now, if you're multiplying 11 by a two-digit number and the sum of its digits is more than 9, just stick the digit in the ones spot of the sum IN the space you made, then carry that extra 1 to the number you started with!

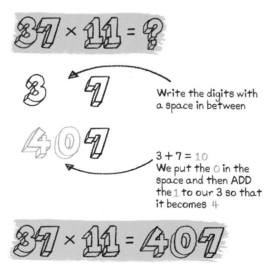

Multiplying by 12 If you're multiplying ANY number by 12, just multiply your original number by 10. Then multiply that original number by 2. Now add the products together, and you're done!

$$12 \times 4 = ?$$

$$10 \times 4 = 40$$ ← First multiply 4 by 10

$$2 \times 4 = 8$$ ← Now multiply 4 by 2

$$40 + 8 = 48$$ ← Then just add those two numbers together

$$12 \times 4 = 48$$ ← BAM!

Multiplying by 0 Are you ready for the biggest multiplication mystery ever?! Kids get stumped by this ALL the time, but YOU are going to become a zero MASTER. Multiplying ANYTHING by zero . . . equals ZERO! Like, ANYTHING.

$$5 \times 0 = 0$$
$$3,346 \times 0 = 0$$
🐱 $\times 0 = 0$ 

Seriously.

Want to know why? Because 5 x 0 actually means "Hey, I have ZERO groups of 5 guys." So, 5s . . . How many groups do you have? ZERO groups! Or, 5 x 0 can also mean "Hey, I have 5 ZERO times." So, like, you actually have no 5s . . . You have ZERO!

Different Ways to Multiply!

There are tons of ways to multiply, and if we covered them all, this book would be, like, a kajillion pages long! Here are some of the best.

Multiplying by 10 or 100 or 1,000: The Step-It-to-the-Left Method

To multiply by 10 or 100 or 1,000 or even 1,000,000,000 (that's a billion!), all you have to do is move each of that number's digits to the left and throw some extra zeros to the right of the last digit.

Q: 26 x 10 = ?

So, 10 has one zero, right? So literally all we have to do is move each digit ONE place-value spot to the left.

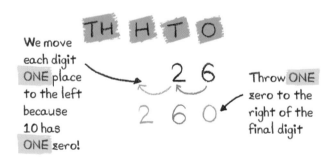

We move each digit ONE place to the left because 10 has ONE zero!

TH H T O

2 6

2 6 0

Throw ONE zero to the right of the final digit

A: 26 x 10 = 260

Watch Out!

I totally mean this: LABEL YOUR PLACE-VALUE COLUMNS! It seriously helps you keep things straight.

Q: 26 x 1,000 = ?

Now we're going to do practically the same thing, except since 1,000 has THREE zeros, we're going to move each digit THREE place-value spots to the left, throw THREE zeros to the right of the last digit, and TA-DA!

A: 26 x 1,000 = 26,000

OMG — You can do it with decimals too! Don't get freaked out just because there's a decimal point — you've got this! It's pretty much the same thing.

Q: 2.6 x 100 = ?

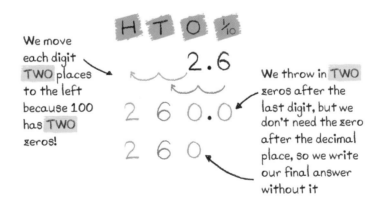

A: 2.6 x 100 = 260

Multiplying by Multiples of 10 or 100 or 1,000

Once you know your times tables and how to multiply by 10 or 100 or 1,000, multiplying by multiples of 10 is super easy! It's another reason to nail those times tables down — as if you needed another one!

Q: 42 x 20 = ?

Step 1: First, break down your multiple of 10. So, 20 breaks into 2 x 10, and our question now looks like this:

$$42 \times 2 \times 10$$

Step 2: Now multiply 42 by 2, so:

$$42 \times 2 = 84$$

Step 3: Finally, we have that 10 left to multiply by! All we have to do when multiplying by 10 is move the digits one place value to the left and plop a zero to the right, sooo . . .

A: 42 x 20 = 840!

You can do the same thing with multiples of 100 and 1,000 — the only diff is that you move more place values to the left and add more zeros, just like in the **Multiplying by 10 or 100 or 1,000** section! And yes — this works with decimals too!

Multiplying Using Place Value

Another cool trick when it comes to multiplying numbers that end in zero is to drop the zero! Basically, you temporarily forget the zero(s) and multiply the remaining digits together. Then count how many zeros were in your original numbers, and THAT'S how many zeros you stick on the end of your final answer! Check it out:

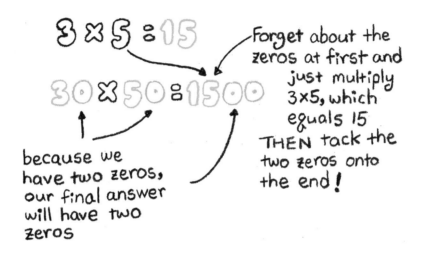

Forget about the zeros at first and just multiply 3×5, which equals 15 THEN tack the two zeros onto the end!

because we have two zeros, our final answer will have two zeros

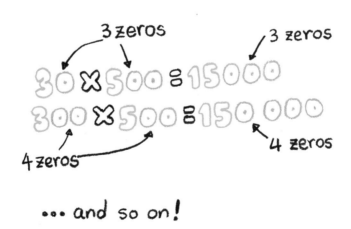

3 zeros

3 zeros

4 zeros

4 zeros

... and so on!

The Real Deal: Short and Long Multiplication!

OMG, so you're at the super-exciting part of your multiplication journey — the part where you learn how to multiply, like, literally ANY number by another one! Kids get scared of long multiplication because it's new and diff — but remember: a lot of the things you LOVE were, once upon a time, new and different. Like, remember when you had NEVER had a freezie before? And then you tried one? AND IT WAS AWESOME? Yep. Think of long multiplication JUST like that! Remember, math is ALL about steps — just follow the steps, go slow, and eventually it will just CLICK!

Starting Off Simple: Short Multiplication

For when you're multiplying a number with more than one digit by a number with just one digit!

Q: 637 x 2 = ?

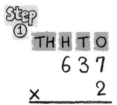

Step 1: Start by writing the number with the most digits on the top and the smaller one underneath. Pay attention to place value! Digits with the same place value must be directly on top of one another!

Step 2: Multiply each of the digits on the top row by 2 — the number on the bottom row. Start on the right with the ones column, and do ONE column at a time, moving left.

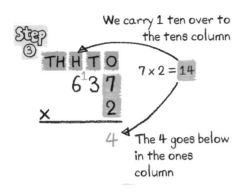

Step
③

We carry 1 ten over to the tens column

TH H T O

6 ³1 3 7

× 2

4

7 × 2 = 14

The 4 goes below in the ones column

Step 3: Multiply your 2 ones by your 7 ones, and voila . . . you have 14 ones! Now, we don't want that 1 ten in the ones column, so carry it over to the tens column by marking a little 1 up there. Stick the 4 under the line in the ones column and move on to the next digit on the left!

Step
④

TH H T O

6 ¹3 7

× 2

7 4

2 × 3 = 6
But remember, we have that extra 1 ten that we carried over from the last step!
6 + 1 = 7

Step 4: Next multiply the 2 by the 3 tens. You know that 2 × 3 = 6, but remember: you have that extra 1 ten that you carried over from the last step, so add that on, giving you 7 tens. Write that under the line in the tens column and move on to the last number on the left!

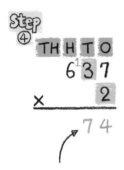

Step
⑤

TH H T O

6 ¹3 7

× 2

1 2 7 4

2 × 6 = 12
We put the 2 in the hundreds column. We put the 1 next door in the thousands column!

Feeling Stuck?!
Think of it this way! Okay, so are you feeling confused about carrying those 1s over everywhere? There IS a reason! 12 hundreds is like saying 10 hundreds + 2 hundreds. So we stick the 2 in the hundreds column, but those extra 10 hundreds are actually equal to 1,000 since 10 × 100 = 1,000! So we exchange 10 hundreds for 1 thousand and put a nice 1 in the thousands column instead because we don't want double digits in any single column!

Step 5: Okay, we are ALMOST done! Finally, multiply the 2 by the 6 in the hundreds column to get 12 hundreds! Put the 2 under the line in the hundreds column and the 1 next to it in the thousands column, and you are done!

A: 637 × 2 = 1,274

For the Pros: Long Multiplication

For when you're multiplying two numbers with ANY number of digits!

Q: 187 x 14 = ?

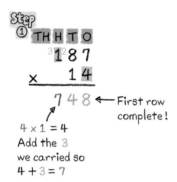

$4 \times 1 = 4$
Add the 3
we carried so
$4 + 3 = 7$

Step 1: Follow the short-multiplication steps from the previous example. Once you've multiplied every digit in the top number by the 4 ones in the bottom number, you've finished your FIRST multiplication row. Time to move on to the next one!

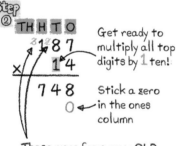

Get ready to multiply all top digits by 1 ten!

Stick a zero in the ones column

Those were from your OLD calculation with the 4 in the ones column. Cross them out so that you don't get confused!

Step 2: All-new step here! Since we have more digits in this question, start a brand new row under the one you just completed so you can multiply all the digits in the top row by 1 ten! You need the new row to record answers. Before you start, stick a 0 in the ones column. Just do it! That zero will help you keep track of your place values. Next, cross out those little numbers you carried over from previous steps, so you don't get confused. But don't erase them — we want to be able to trace our steps!

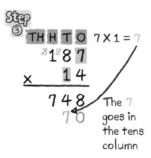

$7 \times 1 = 7$

The 7 goes in the tens column

Step 3: Multiply 1 ten by 7 ones. The answer is 7, so just put your 7 in the tens column. Think of it this way: you're putting your 7 in the first available spot to the left of the zero — that's it!

Step 4: Now multiply that 1 ten by 8 tens. Your answer goes in the first available column to the left, which makes sense! Why? Because 10 x 80 = 800, so we have 8 HUNDREDS!

$1 \times 8 = 8$

We put our 8 in the hundreds column because $10 \times 80 = 800$

Step 5: Next, multiply that 1 ten by the 1 in the hundreds column, and write that down in the next available column to the left! Remember, 10 x 100 = 1,000, which is why that 1 actually ends up in the thousands column — just in case you're wondering!

$1 \times 1 = 1$

We put our 1 in the thousands column because $10 \times 100 = 1000$

Step 6: We're on the final step! Now that you've multiplied all the digits in the number on the top row by all the digits in the number on the bottom row, add your two answer lines together using **column addition**. And then you're done!

A: 187 x 14 = 2,618

Multiplication with Positive and Negative Numbers

The best trick EVER!

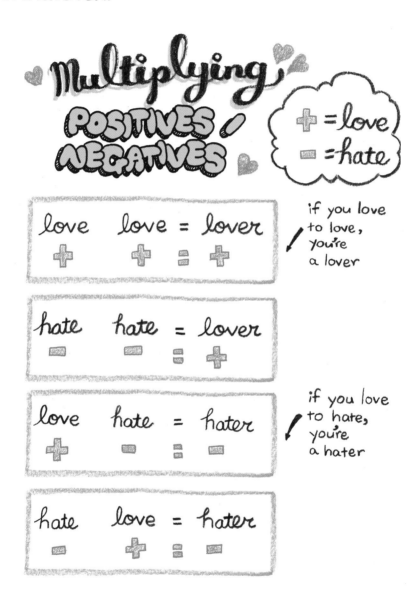

Multiplying POSITIVES NEGATIVES

+ = love
− = hate

| love | love | = | lover |
| + | + | = | + |

if you love to love, you're a lover

| hate | hate | = | lover |
| − | − | = | + |

| love | hate | = | hater |
| + | − | = | − |

if you love to hate, you're a hater

| hate | love | = | hater |
| − | + | = | − |

DIVISION

It's Like Multiplication, but Backwards!

What even is it? There are a bunch of ways to talk about division, but they all just mean the same thing. My two favourite ways to think about it are division as sharing something equally and division as repeated subtraction. Don't worry if you're like, "OMG, what are you saying?" We'll explore these two ways of thinking below, but first, here's some stuff you should know!

Watch out for these keywords! If you see these magic words, they're probably talking about division, so DIVIDE!

how many sets?
DIVIDE BY
HOW MANY GROUPS?
DIVIDE INTO
split up
how many each?

93

Division Is the Opposite of Multiplication

Remember how important it is to know your multiplication facts like a total boss? That's because if you know those, you can use them for division, since multiplication and division are opposites of each other. The numbers follow one pattern when they're being multiplied and the opposite pattern when they're being divided! I like using a rainbow to illustrate this:

$$4 \times 3 = 12 \qquad 12 \div 3 = 4$$

IT'S LIKE A RAINBOW!

When we multiply two factors together, we get a number. When we divide that number by either of those factors, we just get the OTHER factor.

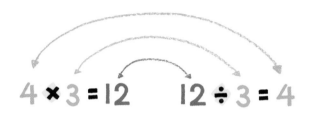

4 and 3 are the factors of 12

$$4 \times 3 = 12$$

$$12 \div 4 = 3 \quad \leftarrow \text{Second Factor}$$
First Factor

$$12 \div 3 = 4 \quad \leftarrow \text{First Factor}$$
Second Factor

You need to know some special division words, so let's learn them first.

Dividend: The number being divided.

Divisor: The number we're dividing by, or how many parts we're dividing our dividend into.

Divisible: When we talk about things being divisible, we're really asking, "Does this number fit into that number with nothing left over?" So, when we're dividing 14 by 7, we say that 14 is divisible by 7 because 7 fits into 14 exactly twice.

Quotient: This is our answer! It's the dividend divided by the divisor. Another way of looking at it is this: We divide our dividend by the divisor. We get a bunch of parts. The value of each of those parts is the quotient.

Remainder: How much is left over once you divide your dividend by your divisor. If something is divisible by another number, there will be NOTHING left over! But sometimes we divide our dividend by our divisor and it doesn't go in perfectly, so we have leftovers. We call those leftovers our remainder.

$$8 \div 2 = 4$$
8 is the dividend
2 is the divisor
4 is the quotient
8 is divisible by 2
There are no remainders!

$$8 \div 3 = 2r2$$
8 is the dividend
3 is the divisor
2 is the quotient
8 is not divisible by 3
There are 2 remainders!

Watch out! Order does matter! Division is like subtraction when it comes to order — it matters, big time! Just ask yourself this: "Is 10 ÷ 2 the same as 2 ÷ 10?" Ummm NO! Even without actually calculating it, you know that those two things are super different. Always remember that you MUST perform division in the order that the numbers appear, so don't move them around!

Division as Repeated Subtraction

Just like we think of multiplication as repeated addition, division is like repeated subtraction. Division is an awesome tool when you need to take one number away from another number over and over again, or take a group of things away from a bigger group of things over and over again.

Let's say you have a pile of 15 gummy bears, and you want to give each of your 3 friends the same amount. You give your first friend 5 of them, your next friend 5 of them, and your third friend 5 of them. You can subtract 5 from 15 exactly 3 times with nothing left over.

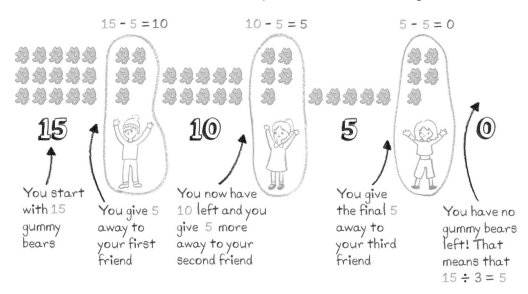

15 - 5 = 10   10 - 5 = 5   5 - 5 = 0

15   **10**   **5**   **0**

You start with 15 gummy bears

You give 5 away to your first friend

You now have 10 left and you give 5 more away to your second friend

You give the final 5 away to your third friend

You have no gummy bears left! That means that 15 ÷ 3 = 5

Division as a Kind of Sharing

Another way to think about division is that it's a kind of sharing, which is handy when you have a thing or a group of things that needs to be split equally. Let's go back to those 15 gummy bears. There are 3 of you, and you want to share those bears equally. If we divide — or share — the 15 gummy bears equally between the 3 of you, each person will get 5 gummy bears!

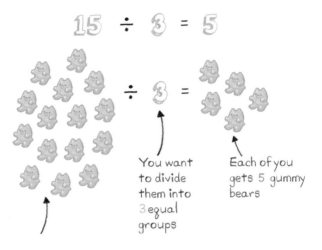

You want to divide them into 3 equal groups

Each of you gets 5 gummy bears

But what if you had 16 gummy bears instead of 15? Your 3 friends would still get 5 gummy bears each, BUT now there is 1 left over for YOU! We call that 1 leftover a **remainder** and in our final answer we put an **r** in front of it, like this: $16 \div 3 = 5r1$

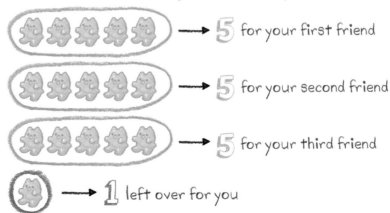

5 for your first friend

5 for your second friend

5 for your third friend

1 left over for you

The Division Tables: Your Secret Weapon!

Here's the deal: division tables are basically just the opposite of times tables. That's it! You can use these tables to help you with your division facts, but my advice is to totally memorize your times tables and then you won't even have to use these division tables. Because division is the exact opposite of multiplication, once you know your multiplication facts, you sort of just KNOW your division facts.

$1 \times 9 = 9$	$9 \div 1 = 9$	$9 \div 9 = 1$
$2 \times 9 = 18$	$18 \div 2 = 9$	$18 \div 9 = 2$
$3 \times 9 = 27$	$27 \div 3 = 9$	$27 \div 9 = 3$
$4 \times 9 = 36$	$36 \div 4 = 9$	$36 \div 9 = 4$
$5 \times 9 = 45$	$45 \div 5 = 9$	$45 \div 9 = 5$
$6 \times 9 = 54$	$54 \div 6 = 9$	$54 \div 9 = 6$
$7 \times 9 = 63$	$63 \div 7 = 9$	$63 \div 9 = 7$
$8 \times 9 = 72$	$72 \div 8 = 9$	$72 \div 9 = 8$
$9 \times 9 = 81$	$81 \div 9 = 9$	$81 \div 9 = 9$
$10 \times 9 = 90$	$90 \div 10 = 9$	$90 \div 9 = 10$
$11 \times 9 = 99$	$99 \div 11 = 9$	$99 \div 9 = 11$
$12 \times 9 = 108$	$108 \div 12 = 9$	$108 \div 9 = 12$

The Division Grid

It's just the multiplication grid you already know and love except things are reversed for division. The numbers we want to divide (the dividends) are in the middle. The numbers on the top and down the far left are our divisors and quotients.

Look familiar? Let's see how the division grid works:

Q: **48 ÷ 6 = ?**

Step ① First, let's find the number we want to divide by. Find that number along the top of the grid. We're looking for 6.

Step ② Trace your finger down the 6 column until you get the number you want to divide, which is 48.

Step ③ Finally, just trace the row that 48 is in allll the way to the left until you hit the wall. THAT number is your answer! Yay 8!

×	1	2	3	4	5	6	7	8	9	10	11	12
1	1	2	3	4	5	6	7	8	9	10	11	12
2	2	4	6	8	10	12	14	16	18	20	22	24
3	3	6	9	12	15	18	21	24	27	30	33	36
4	4	8	12	16	20	24	28	32	36	40	44	48
5	5	10	15	20	25	30	35	40	45	50	55	60
6	6	12	18	24	30	36	42	48	54	60	66	72
7	7	14	21	28	35	42	49	56	63	70	77	84
8	8	16	24	32	40	48	56	64	72	80	88	96
9	9	18	27	36	45	54	63	72	81	90	99	108
10	10	20	30	40	50	60	70	80	90	100	110	120
11	11	22	33	44	55	66	77	88	99	110	121	132
12	12	24	36	48	60	72	84	96	108	120	132	144

A: **48 ÷ 6 = 8**

It's OK! Some people like to look for their divisor on the far left instead of the top row, and then find their quotient on the top row instead of the far left! Both ways give you the same result.

Division Hacks to Impress Your Friends!

The best way to divide quickly in your head is to know your times tables. Seriously, they're that important. But you can also use tricks to remember stuff, so here are some of the coolest division hacks around. Once you know these shortcuts, you'll be able to look at a number and easily figure out what it's divisible by.

You can tell if a number is divisible by	if	Like these numbers!
2	Its last digit is an even number.	4, 16, 20, 298, 538, 290 are all divisible by 2.
3	If you add all of the digits in the number together, and their sum is divisible by 3.	24 $2 + 4 = 6$ 6 is divisible by 3 because $6 \div 3 = 2$ So 24 is divisible by 3!
4	Check out the last two digits of the number. Is the number that THEY form is divisible by 4 with no remainder, then the original number is divisible by 4.	624 The last two digits are 24 $24 \div 4 = 6$, with no remainder. So 624 is divisible by 4!
5	Its last digit is either 0 or 5.	75, 6,785, 670, 10 are all divisible by 5. Easy!
6	There are two things to look for. First, the number needs to be even. If it is, then add all of its digits together and see if their sum is divisible by 3. If it is, you're good to go.	1,524 The last digit is 4, an even number. So now we can keep going: $1 + 5 + 2 + 4 = 12$ 12 is divisible by 3. So 1,524 is divisible by 6!

You can tell if a number is divisible by	if	Like these numbers!
7	This is weird, but it works. Take the last digit and remove it from the rest of the digits. Multiply it by 2. Now subtract it from the number that the remaining digits form. If that result is divisible by 7, then so is your original number!	651 Separate the 1 from the 65 so you have 65 and 1 Now multiply: $1 \times 2 = 2$ Subtract: $65 - 2 = 63$ $63 \div 7 = 9$ So 651 is divisible by 7!
8	This works for bigger numbers. Check out the last three digits of the number. Is it divisible by 8 with no remainder? Then so is your original number.	1,248 The last three digits are 248 248 is divisible by 8 because $248 \div 8 = 31$ So 1,248 is divisible by 8!
9	Add all the digits in the number together until you are down to a single digit. If that sum is 9, then the original number is divisible by 9. With this hack, you may have to add the digits together more than once to get a single-digit answer.	1,665 $1 + 6 + 6 + 5 = 18$ $1 + 8 = 9$ So 1,665 is divisible by 9!
10	Its last digit will be zero.	50; 8,970; 1,232,980 are all divisible by 10!

You can tell if a number is divisible by	if	Like these numbers!
11	This one is tricky, but it works. You need to subtract and add digits in an alternating pattern. Start by subtracting the second digit from the first, then add the following digit, then subtract the NEXT digit, and so on. Then check if that answer is divisible by 11.	2,816 $2 - 8 = -6$ $-6 + 1 = -5$ $-5 - 6 = -11$ -11 is divisible by 11, so then 2816 is as well. If you get zero as your answer using this method, remember 0 is divisible by 11 because 0 is divisible by anything.
12	If your number is divisible by 3 and then that answer is divisible by 4, then you know that it's also divisible by 12. Check out the divisibility rules for 3 and 4 and use those.	168 $168 \div 3 = 56$ $56 \div 4 = 14$ So 168 is divisible by 12!

Dividing with Zero

This is legit one of the biggest mysteries of all time. What's the deal? **Zero divided by ANYTHING is still zero!**

$$0 \div 5 = 0$$
$$0 \div 3,547 = 0$$
$$0 \div \text{🧁} = 0$$

Just like with multiplication, when we divide zero by anything, the answer is zero. It makes sense if you think about it! If you have zero gumballs and you try to divide them up into groups ... ummm you can't? Since you had zero to start with, you can make zero groups. You still got nothing!

ANYTHING divided by zero is undefined!

$$5 \div 0 = \text{undefined}$$
$$3{,}478 \div 0 = \text{undefined}$$
$$\text{🧁} \div 0 = \text{undefined}$$

Okay, so here's the mistake MOST kids make: they think that dividing by zero equals zero, just like multiplying by zero. But that's not how it works. Think about it this way: Division is splitting something into equal parts or groups. Say you have 12 gummies and you want to share them among 3 friends. How are you going to divide them up? Easy!

Your 12 gummies

Your 12 gummies divided among your 3 friends.

Now, pretend you had those 12 gummies again, and you wanted to divide them up among **zero** people. How many does each person get? Does that question even make sense? NO! It makes zero sense — LOL! But for real, it doesn't make sense — so we can't do it. And that's why dividing by zero is undefined. When we try to divide by zero, things stop making sense. So we don't do it.

Different Ways to Divide

Some people like bananas in their peanut butter sandwiches, while others like jam. Or both! The point is, just as there are many ways to eat PB sandwiches, there are many ways to divide. Here are a couple — if you find one that works for you, go for it.

Before you start You should have a decimal point in your number just in case. If your dividend is a **whole number** and doesn't already have one, just stick one to the right of its last digit. I like to use place-value labels so that things don't get too crazy.

Dividing by 10 or 100 or 1,000: The Step-It-to-the-Right Method

Remember our step-it-to-the-left method when we were multiplying? Well, this is just the exact opposite. When dividing, we step-it-to-the-RIGHT. To divide by 10 or 100 or 1,000 or even 1,000,000,000, all you have to do is move each of the number's digits to the right by the number of zeros in your divisor.

Starting off simple:

Q: 7,341 ÷ 10 = ?

Okay, so 10 has ONE zero, right? So literally ALL we have to do is move each digit ONE place-value spot to the right — that's seriously it! Since 7,341 is a whole number, don't forget to put that decimal point at the end of your dividend before you begin!

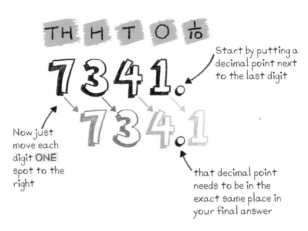

Since dividing by 10 means that every single digit will be 10 TIMES smaller, it makes sense for us to move each digit to the right, to a place value that is ALSO 10 times smaller! Just like that!

A: 7,341 ÷ 10 = 734.1

Let's do another one ...

Q: 7,341 ÷ 100 = ?

Now we're going to do practically the same thing, except since 100 has TWO zeros, we're going to move each digit TWO place-value spots to the right.

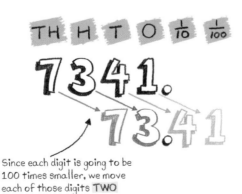

A: 7,341 ÷ 100 = 73.41

... and one more!

Q: 73 ÷ 1,000 = ?

You can do the same sort of thing when you divide by numbers like 1,000 too — all you do is keep moving more and more place-value spots to the right depending on how many zeros you have!

Don't freak! Sometimes when you divide a smallish number by a waaaay bigger number, you might get some empty spaces between your decimal point and the first digit of your answer. No biggie, just fill those in with zeros.

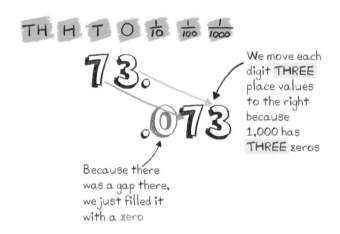

We move each digit **THREE** place values to the right because 1,000 has **THREE** zeros

Because there was a gap there, we just filled it with a zero

A: 73 ÷ 1,000 = .073

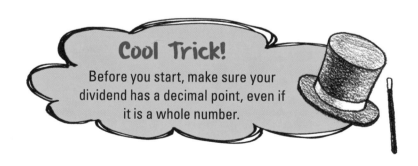

Cool Trick!
Before you start, make sure your dividend has a decimal point, even if it is a whole number.

Dividing by Multiples of 10 or 100 or 1,000!

Once you know your division tables and know how to divide by 10 or 100 or 1,000, dividing by multiples of 10 — like 20 or 300 or 4,000 — is super easy. For this hack to work, you want to make sure that BOTH your dividend and divisor are multiples of 10 or 100 or 1,000!

Q: 3,600 ÷ 40 = ?

Step 1: Let's think of this question as 3,600 ÷ (10 x 4), then break that apart.

Step 2: So, what's 3,600 divided by 10? You know it (since we just learned the hack for dividing by 10)! Move all of the digits ONE place value to the right.

$$3,600 \div 10 = 360$$

Step 3: Now, just divide 360 by 4. You can figure it out! 36 ÷ 4 = 9, so it makes sense that:

$$360 \div 4 = 90$$

And we are *FINITO!*

A: 3,600 ÷ 40 = 90

More multiples!

There's more on dividing multiples and other cool info that will help you with division here:
www.scholastic.ca/math-hacks

Dividing Any Time, Anywhere, by Anything!

I'm going to show you how to work out division with numbers of any size. That's right — using this method, you'll be able to divide the craziest numbers you can think of like a superstar!

Start off simple — one-digit divisors

Q: $193 \div 8 = ?$

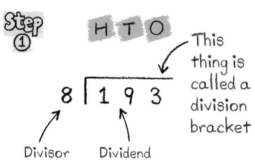

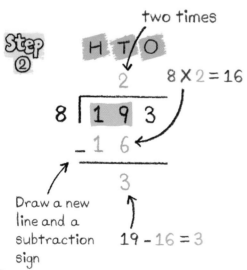

Step 1: Okay, let's start with the basics! Draw yourself a nice long-division bracket — it sort of looks like if you pushed the letter "L" over, onto its face. Write the dividend under the bracket and the divisor on the left, outside the bracket.

Step 2: Start by trying to divide the first digit of your dividend by the divisor. Remember, you're looking for it to divide evenly, meaning the entire 8 — not just a piece of it — fits in the 1 at least once. In this case it doesn't, so look at the second digit of the dividend as well. Does 8 fit into 19? Yes! It fits into 19 two times. Write the 2 on top of the bracket, right above the 9. Then, because 8 fits into 19 twice, multiply 8 by 2 and write the result, 16, right under the 19. Draw a new line and a subtraction sign, as though you're about to do column subtraction . . . because you are! Now subtract 16 from 19 and write the answer under that new line.

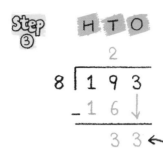

Step ③

Step 3: Bring the next digit in the dividend down to sit under the new line you just drew. It goes next to the friendly 3, turning it into 33.

We bring the 3 down

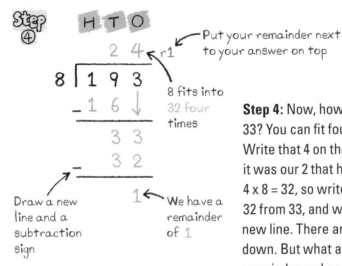

Put your remainder next to your answer on top

8 fits into 32 four times

Draw a new line and a subtraction sign

We have a remainder of 1

Step 4: Now, how many times does 8 go into 33? You can fit four 8s into 33, with a 1 leftover. Write that 4 on the bracket above the 3, because it was our 2 that helped us get that 4. We know 4 x 8 = 32, so write that under the 33. Subtract 32 from 33, and write the answer under another new line. There are no more digits left to bring down. But what about that leftover 1? It's a remainder and part of the answer, so write it on top of the division bracket as **r1**. Hey — you just did long division!

A: 193 ÷ 8 = 24r1

Feeling stuck? Think times tables!

Even though we're talking division here, make sure you're totally up to speed on your multiplication. Practise those times tables if you need to. Knowing them by heart will help you here — and lots of other math places too!

Time to Level Up!

Let's try a bigger divisor so that you can see how good you are at this! Once you know how to do it, the size of the numbers doesn't even matter.

Freaking out? Remember, just because something takes longer or has more steps, it doesn't mean that it's actually harder. Often, steps repeat themselves, so you're not actually doing a million new things. You're just doing what you already know, only a few more times.

Q: 6,285 ÷ 26 = ?

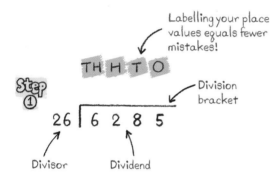

Labelling your place values equals fewer mistakes!

Division bracket

Divisor   Dividend

Step 1: Set it up! Draw the division bracket, write the dividend under it, and then write the divisor outside the bracket on the left.

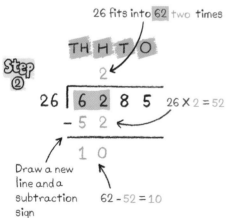

26 fits into 62 two times

26 X 2 = 52

Draw a new line and a subtraction sign

62 - 52 = 10

Step 2: Try to divide the first digit of your dividend by 26. Remember, you're looking for it to divide evenly, which means the entire 26 fits in the 6 at least once. It doesn't, so look at the second digit of the dividend as well. Can we divide 62 by 26? Yes, we can! Since 26 fits into 62 twice, write a 2 on top of the bracket RIGHT above the second digit in the dividend. Then, multiply 26 by 2, and write "52" under the 62. Draw a new line for your column subtraction, and take away 52 from 62. Write the answer (10!) underneath.

Step 3: Bring down the next digit in the dividend to sit beside the 10. It becomes 108.

We bring the 8 down

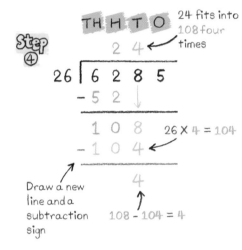

24 fits into 108 four times

26 X 4 = 104

Draw a new line and a subtraction sign

108 - 104 = 4

Step 4: Let's divide that 108 by 26! Our friend 26 goes into 108 four times, so write "4" above the division bracket, directly over the 8. Just like step 2, multiply 26 x 4 and write the answer, 104, under the 108. Now draw another subtraction line and sign, and subtract 104 from 108. Write the answer, 4, under that line.

Feeling stuck? That's okay — just figure it out!

It's totally normal to not know off the top of your head how many times 26 fits into 108. Just figure it out! You know when it says "show your work" on a test? This is the sort of thing that means. Take a look at the 26 and the 108. How many times will it fit? Take a guess. Maybe three times? Work out what 26 x 3 is. How close is 78 to 108? Subtract them. In this case, you get 30. That's enough room to fit in one more 26.

Step 5: Bring down the next digit in the dividend (5!) and turn that 4 into a 45.

Bring the 5 down and place it next to the 4

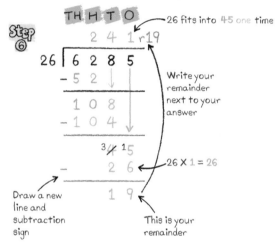

26 fits into 45 one time

Write your remainder next to your answer

26 X 1 = 26

Draw a new line and subtraction sign

This is your remainder

Step 6: Divide 45 by 26. You got this! Okay, 26 goes into 45 once, so let's put a 1 above the division bracket on top of the 5. Subtract 26 from 45. Write your answer, 19, under another line. There are no more digits left to bring down, so you're almost done . . . almost! What do we do with that 19? Remember, it's a remainder, so write it as part of your answer, on top of the division bracket. And now you are actually done.

A: 6,285 ÷ 26 = 241r19

Dealing with Remainders

Sometimes when you have a division question, your divisor goes into your dividend a perfect number of times. Other times, you've got a number left over and we call it a **remainder**. Just like leftover pizza, you can store that remainder in different ways.

You can put pizza back in the box, wrap it in foil or stick it in a reusable container. Fractions, decimals and the leftover numbers with an "r" in front of them are different ways to store remainders. But how do know which one to use? Check the question or ask your teacher to find out which way to store your remainder.

Here are a couple ways to convert remainders into decimals or fractions. Don't worry . . . they're all easy!

Converting Remainders into Decimals

All we're really doing with this is continuing to divide using long division, by adding magic zeros! You actually already know how to do this.

Q: 92 ÷ 8 = ?

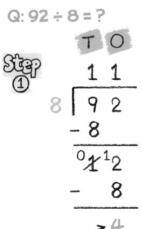

Our remainder was 4

Step 1: We've fast-forwarded here, to the point where we've found out that our remainder is 4. But, instead of writing it on top of the division bracket next to our answer, we want to convert it into a decimal.

Add a new place value column and label it

Extend your division bracket

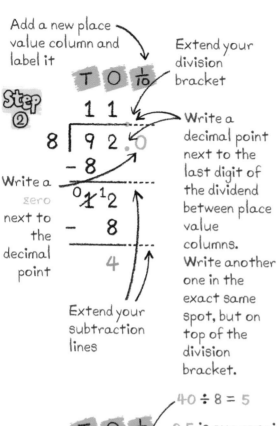

Step ②

T O ⅒

1 1

8 ⟌ 9 2 . 0

− 8

⁰𝟙¹2

− 8

4

Write a zero next to the decimal point

Extend your subtraction lines

Write a decimal point next to the last digit of the dividend between place value columns. Write another one in the exact same spot, but on top of the division bracket.

Step 2: Extend your division bracket and all of your lines. You need more room! Put a decimal point to the right of the last digit of the dividend, then place a zero next to that. Remember, that doesn't change its value. Now place a decimal point on top of the division bracket. Put it next to your answer and right above the decimal point you just wrote in. They should be exactly in line with each other.

40 ÷ 8 = 5

Step ③

T O ⅒

1 1 5

8 ⟌ 9 2 . 0

− 8

⁰𝟙¹2

− 8

4 0

− 4 0

0

0.5 is our remainder as a decimal. We don't need to put an r next to it if we've turned it into a decimal.

Bring the zero down

8 X 5 = 40

We have no remainder left so we're done!

Draw a new line and subtraction symbol

Step 3: Bring that zero down so it's next to the remainder of 4, turning it into 40. Divide 40 by 8 and you get 5. Write that 5 on top of the division bracket, to the right of your decimal point, in the tenths column. Now, because 8 x 5 = 40, subtract that 40 from the 40 already sitting there. Answer: 0, zero, *nada*, nothing. There is no part of the remainder left — and we are done.

A: 92 ÷ 8 = 11.5

Converting Remainders into Fractions

This is super easy! All we have to do is write the remainder as a numerator on top of the divisor, which becomes our denominator. Literally, that is it. If you need the low-down on fractions first, just turn the page!

Q: $92 \div 8 = ?$

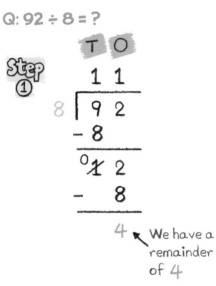

Step 1: Let's skip ahead. We're at the point where we can see that we have a remainder of 4, so let's turn that into a fraction.

We have a remainder of 4

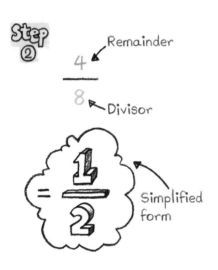

Remainder

Divisor

Simplified form

Step 2: Make a fraction. Throw that remainder on top of the divisor. Can it be simplified? Then you are done. Now remember, this isn't our remainder — it's the remainder translated into a fraction, so don't write an r next to the ½. Instead we just write the ½ as part of the answer!

A: $92 \div 8 = 11\frac{1}{2}$

FRACTIONS

Half the Work You Think They Are!

I get it . . . fractions can seem totally scary, but they're actually awesome! Would you rather have one piece of cake or one and a half pieces of cake? If you chose the second option, guess what? You love fractions!

What even are they? Up until now, we've been mostly talking about **whole numbers**, which are nice and neat. Fractions are made up of either a piece of a number, or a whole number plus a piece of another number. They can be part of one thing (like half of one piece of cake) or part of a group of things (like half of the kids in your class). Not so bad, right?

A fraction is one number written on top of another number, just like this:

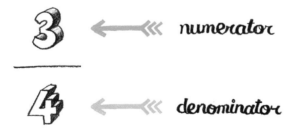

$$\frac{3}{4} \quad \begin{matrix} \leftarrow \text{numerator} \\ \\ \leftarrow \text{denominator} \end{matrix}$$

We call the top part the **numerator.** It's the number of parts we have. The bottom is the **denominator.** It's the number of parts the whole thing was EQUALLY divided into in the first place.

You know that little fraction line? The " / " is another way of writing a division symbol (the " ÷ " sign!), which is also known as an obelus!

Let's break it down:

$$10 / 2 = 5 \qquad 10 \div 2 = 5$$

we can say
"10 over 2"

OR

We can say
"10 divided by 2"

You can make any whole number into a fraction by putting it over a 1:

6 is the same as $6/1$

Check out this delish pizza. It's been cut into 4 equal parts, which we call **quarters** (more about that later!). If you ate 3 of those pieces, you would have eaten 3 **quarters**, or ¾, of the pizza and you would be really full. Another way of seeing it is 3 parts out of a possible 4 parts.

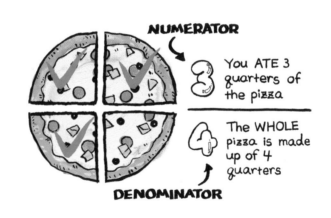

NUMERATOR

3 — You ATE 3 quarters of the pizza

4 — The WHOLE pizza is made up of 4 quarters

DENOMINATOR

Cool Trick!
If you have trouble remembering which goes where, just think "DOWNominator" — it's the one down at the bottom.

What's the Deal with Fractions?

The coolest thing about fractions is that they can help you divide something into as many equal parts as you want. Fractions are all about equality! The pizza on page 117 had been divided into 4 equal parts. What's even better is that depending on how many people you invite to your party, you can cut that pizza into as many equal pieces as you need using your new secret weapon: FRACTIONS!

2 slices - halves
Two people get 1/2 each :D

3 slices - thirds
Three people get 1/3 each :)

4 slices - quarters
Four people get 1/4 each :l

5 slices - fifths
Five people get 1/5 each :/

6 slices - sixths
Six people get 1/6 each :C

7 slices - sevenths
Seven people get 1/7 each D:

Notice that the larger the denominator is, the smaller those pieces are. That's because the denominator is telling us how many pieces the whole is divided into, or how many people are at your party. The more pieces we divide something into, the smaller they have to be.

Unit fractions – what?

Relax! These are just fractions where the numerator is the number 1. It's easy to compare the value of unit fractions because all you have to do is look at the denominator. The bigger the denominator, the smaller the value of the fraction – just think of the pizza. Obviously ½ is bigger than ⅒, because ½ means you're getting a whole half of the pizza. Yes, please!

Whole fractions – what?

If you have the same number as the numerator and denominator, it's always a whole! That means the entire fraction actually just equals 1. Remember how fractions are just the top divided by the bottom? Let's think about it ... ⁶⁄₆ really just means 6 ÷ 6, which equals 1. Or 1,234,567 ÷ 1,234,567 = 1. Or whatever!

Equivalent fractions – what?

Equivalent fractions are worth the exact same as each other, even though they might look different. But how does that even work? Well, when you multiply or divide both the numerator and denominator by the same number, the fraction keeps its value. Remember whole fractions? They're just 1 in disguise! Here's how to make an equivalent fraction:

Q: ⅔ x ⅘ = ?

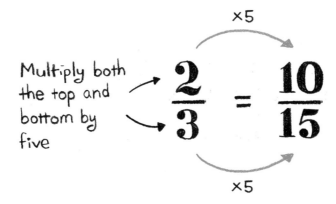

×5

Multiply both the top and bottom by five

$$\frac{2}{3} = \frac{10}{15}$$

×5

119

A: ⅔ x ⅘ = ¹⁰⁄₁₅ which is an equivalent fraction!

It works the other way — with division — too, because ¼ equals 1.

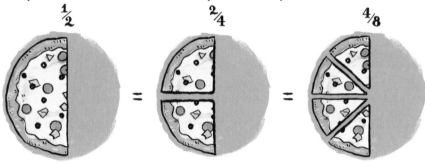

And if equivalent fractions were pizza, they'd look like this:

Simplifying Fractions — What Is That?

Remember how when we learned about **equivalent fractions**, we found that when we divided the numerator and denominator by the same number, the fraction's value stayed the same? Well, that's all simplifying is! If we keep dividing the numerator and denominator by the same number until we can't go any farther, we have **simplified** the fraction — we've basically made it as basic as possible. This is also called **reducing your fraction.**

On your marks! Once you've learned the basics of fractions, your teacher will TOTALLY want to see you reduce your fractions for homework and tests. This is the proper form for your answer . . . and it's worth marks!

Start off simple:

Q: Write $\frac{6}{12}$ in its simplest form.

Step 1: What common factors do the numerator and denominator share? In this case, both 6 and 12 are divisible by 3, so 3 is a common factor.

Step 2: Divide both the numerator and denominator by 3, and you get $\frac{2}{4}$.

Step 3: Hmmm . . . it looks like the numerator and denominator still have a common factor, which means that the fraction isn't in its simplest form. They're both still divisible by 2, so you have to divide again.

Step 4: Divide your new numerator and denominator by 2, and you get ½.

Step 5: When are you done? Once your numerator and denominator have nothing else in common (so sad!), your fraction is officially in its simplest form. 1 and 2 are not evenly divisible by anything else, so you are DONE!

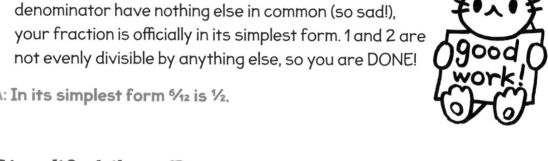

A: In its simplest form ⁶⁄₁₂ is ½.

Simplify Like a Pro

There's an even faster way to simplify! All you have to do is find the **greatest common factor** (the biggest one!) that your numerator and denominator share, divide them both by that magic number, and BAM! Your fraction is instantly simplified in two steps. When you're choosing what to divide the top and bottom of your fraction by, really think about it. You ONLY want to choose factors of each number. If you don't, you'll get a decimal. Decimals are awesome, but we don't want them here.

Q: Write ⁸⁄₁₂ in its simplest form.

Step 1: Instead of choosing any common factor, like 2, let's choose the greatest one, which is 4!

Step 2: Divide the numerator and denominator by 4, and you get ⅔. You are DONE. Your numerator and denominator have nothing left in common, therefore your fraction is in its simplest form.

A: ⁸⁄₁₂ in its simplest form is ⅔!

Feeling stuck? Think of it this way!
If you're having trouble figuring out what to divide the top and bottom by, make sure you totally understand what **common factors** are all about. Head over to page 76 in Multiplication. It really helps to know your times — and division — tables!

So Many Fractions

There are three types of fraction that you will meet on your mathematical journey. There are **proper fractions**, **improper fractions** and **mixed fractions**. You gotta know them all!

There are three types of fraction:

Smaller → $\dfrac{5}{9}$ ← Larger

PROPER FRACTION

Larger (or equal) → $\dfrac{5}{3}$ ← Smaller (or equal)

IMPROPER FRACTION

$2\dfrac{1}{5}$

MIXED FRACTION

Proper Fractions

Just like the name suggests, this guy is nice and tidy. The value of a proper fraction is always less than 1, with a numerator that is smaller than the denominator, like this:

Improper Fractions

These fractions are totally cheeky! Improper fractions have a numerator that is bigger than the denominator, like this:

When the numerator and denominator are the exact same, like this whole number in disguise, it's also considered an improper fraction. Improper fractions always have a value that is 1 or more.

Mixed Fractions

A mixed fraction is made up of both a whole number and a fraction. Sometimes they're called mixed numbers. Either way, we LOVE them!

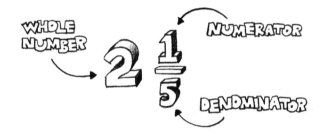

Changing Improper Fractions into Mixed Fractions!

We turn improper fractions into mixed fractions because we love the simplest form ... so, how does it work?

Q: What is 9/2 as a mixed fraction?

Step 1: Divide the numerator by the denominator as far as it will go — so, how many times can that denominator fit into the numerator nicely?

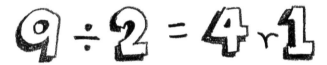

Step 2: That 4 becomes your nice whole number. Now take whatever's left, in this case a 1, stick it over the original denominator ... and you're done!

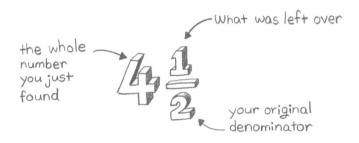

the whole number you just found

What was left over

your original denominator

A: 9/2 as a fraction number is 4 ½.

Changing Mixed Fractions into Improper Fractions!

It works both ways. Sometimes we WANT to turn a mixed fraction into an improper fraction.

Q: What is 2 ⅓ as an improper fraction?

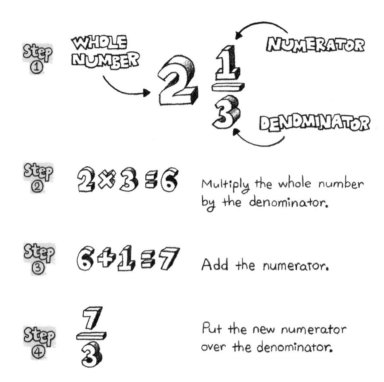

Step ① WHOLE NUMBER 2 ⅓ NUMERATOR DENOMINATOR

Step ② 2 × 3 = 6 — Multiply the whole number by the denominator.

Step ③ 6 + 1 = 7 — Add the numerator.

Step ④ $\frac{7}{3}$ — Put the new numerator over the denominator.

A: 2 ⅓ as an improper fraction is ⁷⁄₃.

Common Denominators

What even are they? Fractions with common denominators have the same denominator. You'll need common denominators for comparing, adding, subtracting and doing other cool stuff. If you don't have two fractions with the same denominator, you need to figure it out! Good thing there are several ways to do this.

Common Denominators — The Easy Way

Q: Which is bigger: ⅔ or ⅗?

Which of these fractions is larger? Sort of hard to tell, right? That's because they have different denominators. If you multiply each one by a whole-number fraction made up of the other's denominator, you'll have an instant **common denominator.**

×5

Multiply both the top and bottom by 5 → $\dfrac{2}{3} = \dfrac{10}{15}$

×5

Step 1: Multiply the first fraction by the other fraction's denominator. So, you're going to multiply both the top and bottom of ⅔ by 5, because that's the denominator of our good friend ⅗.

× 3

Multiply the top and bottom by 3 → $\dfrac{3}{5} = \dfrac{9}{15}$

× 3

Step 2: Now we've got to do the same thing to ⅗ because, hey, that's only fair! Remember, our goal is to get the same denominator. This time you're going to multiply both the top and bottom of ⅗ by 3, because that's the denominator of our good friend ⅔.

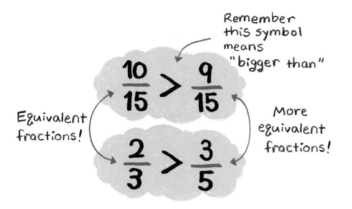

Remember this symbol means "bigger than"

Equivalent fractions!

More equivalent fractions!

$$\frac{10}{15} > \frac{9}{15}$$

$$\frac{2}{3} > \frac{3}{5}$$

Step 3: Now we have two fractions that we can compare because the denominators are the same. Remember that $\frac{2}{3}$ and $\frac{10}{15}$ are equivalent fractions; so are $\frac{3}{5}$ and $\frac{9}{15}$. We can totally see that $\frac{2}{3} > \frac{3}{5}$!

A: $\frac{2}{3} > \frac{3}{5}$

Common Denominators – The LCD Way

Okay, so I showed you the easy way to find common denominators, but sometimes you may find your result isn't in the simplest form – and we like our fractions to be fully simplified! Here's a pretty sweet way to make sure that your fractions always end up that way.

Q: Which is bigger: $\frac{3}{4}$ or $\frac{7}{10}$?

Again, it's hard to tell which is bigger, right? Sure, you can multiply $\frac{3}{4}$ by 10 and $\frac{7}{10}$ by 4 to find out, and that totally works. But there's another way and you need to know it! We're going to use something we call the **lowest common denominator,** otherwise known as the LCD – because it sounds cooler.

Step 1: To find the LCD, you need to find the **lowest common multiple** (LCM!) of the two denominators. So, let's use a number line for 4 and for 10 … and we can see that 20 is actually the LCM of 4 and 10, so it becomes the LCD.

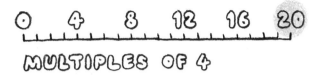

MULTIPLES OF 4

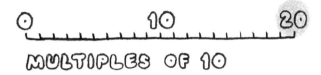

MULTIPLES OF 10

Step 2: Now, rewrite the fractions with their new denominator of 20. Divide the new denominator by each fraction's original denominator and then multiply both the top and bottom by that magic number. How do we find our magic number? You just divide the new denominator by the old one. Here, we divide 20 by 4 and see that the magic number IS in fact 5!

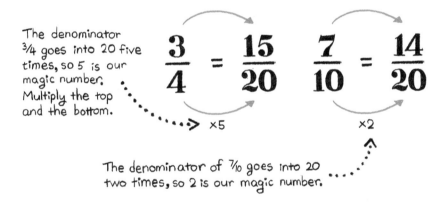

The denominator ¾ goes into 20 five times, so 5 is our magic number. Multiply the top and the bottom.

$$\frac{3}{4} = \frac{15}{20} \qquad \frac{7}{10} = \frac{14}{20}$$

×5   ×2

The denominator of ⁷⁄₁₀ goes into 20 two times, so 2 is our magic number.

Step 3: Now we have two fractions that we can actually compare, and REMEMBER, because ¾ and ¹⁵⁄₂₀ are the same thing and because ⁷⁄₁₀ and ¹⁴⁄₂₀ are the same thing (*cough cough* hello, equivalent fractions!), we can happily conclude that ¾ > ⁷⁄₁₀!

A: ¾ > ⁷⁄₁₀

Fractions in ACTION!

Now that we're all pros with fractions, it's time to actually do math with them. These hacks will help you add, subtract, multiply and divide fractions like a boss. BUT before you do any sort of operation with your fractions, you should turn any whole numbers or mixed fractions into improper fractions. That's why improper fractions rock! Most of the time, converting those cheeky whole numbers or mixed fractions to improper fractions is always the first step.

$$\text{NO!} \qquad\qquad \text{YES!}$$
$$2\,\tfrac{1}{4} \times \tfrac{2}{3} \;\rightarrow\; \tfrac{9}{4} \times \tfrac{2}{3}$$

Remember these two tips:

Before you start: no mixed fractions or whole numbers allowed!

Before you end: simplify improper fraction answers into mixed numbers!

Adding Fractions

The number one thing to know before adding fractions? Your fractions HAVE to have the same denominator. Have to!

Q: $\tfrac{5}{3} + \tfrac{1}{2} = ?$

Step 1: Okay, we're good: no mixed fractions or whole numbers. But our denominators aren't the same! So, we need to find our **lowest common denominator** and rewrite them. Here, the LCD is 6!

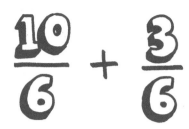

Step 2: Add the new numerators together but DO NOT touch the denominators. Just stick the total on top of the denominator, and we're good to go!

$$\frac{10}{6} + \frac{3}{6} = \frac{13}{6}$$

Step 3: Rewrite the answer in its simplest form by turning that improper fraction into a mixed fraction, and we are DONE!

A: ⁵⁄₃ + ½ = 2 ⅙

Subtracting Fractions

The good news is that once you know how to add fractions, subtracting fractions is a piece of cake. Just like with adding fractions, no whole numbers or mixed fractions allowed, and the denominators have to be the same. Let's do this!

Q: ⅔ – ⅗ = ?

Step 1: Uh-oh, our denominators aren't the same. So, find your **lowest common denominator** and rewrite both fractions. Here, the LCD is 15.

$$10/15 - 9/15$$

Step 2: Subtract the second numerator from the first, but DO NOT touch the denominators. Just stick the difference on top of the denominator, and we're good to go!

A: $2/3 - 3/5 = 1/15$

Multiplying Fractions

Multiplication is actually the easiest operation to do with fractions, ever. You don't even need a common denominator! Remember, we still don't want any mixed fractions or whole numbers. Ready?

Q: $5/3 \times 1/2 = ?$

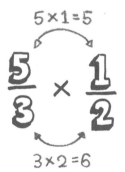

$5 \times 1 = 5$

$$\frac{5}{3} \times \frac{1}{2}$$

$3 \times 2 = 6$

Step 1: Seriously, ALL we have to do is multiply the top by the top, the bottom by the bottom, and ta-da!

$$= \frac{5}{6}$$

Step 2: Okay, there's no official second step, but if your answer isn't in its simplest form, you need to DO THAT NOW!

A: $5/3 \times 1/2 = 5/6$

Dividing Fractions

Division with fractions may seem weird and impossible, but it's super easy — stick with me! When you've got fractions and need to divide, flip the second fraction and multiply. Like this:

Q: ⅝ ÷ ½ = ?

Step 1: Take that ½ and turn it upside down!

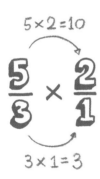

Step 2: Now all we're doing is multiplying fractions. Multiply the top by the top, the bottom by the bottom, and voila!

Step 3: Eeeep! Remember to simplify — turn this guy into a mixed fraction . . . and now we have our final answer.

A: ⅝ ÷ ½ = 3 ⅓

DECIMALS

Connecting the Dots . . . on Decimal Points

What even are they? Just like fractions, **decimal numbers** are made up of whole numbers and pieces of numbers. A dot, called a **decimal point**, is what separates the whole number part from the fraction part of the decimal number. Check it out:

Whole numbers go to the left of the decimal point

Fractions go to the right of the decimal point

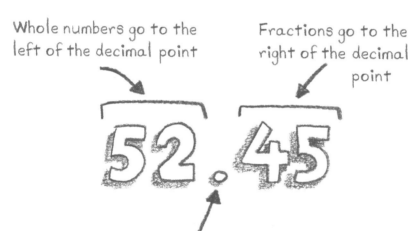

This is called a decimal point. It separates the whole part of the number from the fraction part

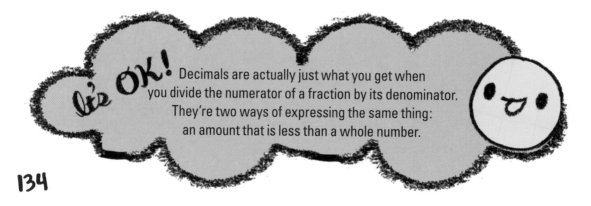

It's OK! Decimals are actually just what you get when you divide the numerator of a fraction by its denominator. They're two ways of expressing the same thing: an amount that is less than a whole number.

Decoding Decimals

Place Value — This Time with Decimals

Remember how you totally killed that whole place value thing in the Numbers chapter? Well, now you're going to do it again, but we're going to throw decimals into the mix. A little dot, just like a period, represents the decimal point.

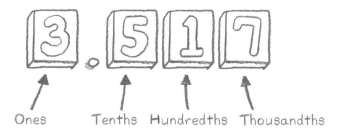

Ones   Tenths Hundredths Thousandths

Our new friend 3.517 has 3 **decimal places.**

Wait, what? A digit's position after the decimal point is what we call its decimal place. So, 3.5 has one decimal place and 3.517 has three decimal places. But don't confuse decimal place with value. They are two different things. The number 5.3 has one decimal place, but it's still bigger than 4.79 because its most significant digit is higher: 5 > 4.

Say It Out Loud!

To say a decimal number out loud, try this:

1. Say the whole-number part of it first, using the tricks from page 44 in the Numbers chapter.

2. When you get to the decimal point, say the word "and." This is why we don't say "and" for any other part of the number — we save it for the decimal point!

3. Read the part after the decimal point like a regular number, but add **"ths"** to whatever place value the last number belongs to. Like this:

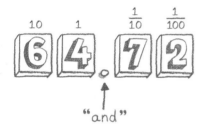

So you'd say "sixty-four AND seventy-two hundredths."

Fast Hack!
Write "DP" instead of decimal point when you're doing your work.

Comparing Decimal Numbers

Okay, so how can you tell which number is the biggest? The value of decimal places works just like whole-number place value. The farther they are to the left, the more value they have. The farther they are to the right, the less value they have. We compare decimals using the exact same steps we use to compare whole numbers.

Step 1: Line up the numbers on top of each other, making sure that every digit is in the right place-value position. Label the place-value positions to keep things organized.

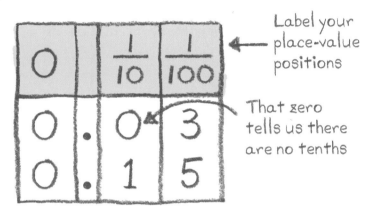

Label your place-value positions

That zero tells us there are no tenths

Step 2: Compare the digits with the highest place value first. Remember, that means we start from the left. The leftmost column is the ones column. The digits in the ones column are both zero, so we move right and compare the tenths column. Since 1 is bigger than zero, we don't need to keep going. The winner is 0.15!

A: 0.15 is the bigger number!

Zero is a trickster! Unlike with whole numbers, placing zeros at the very end (farthest right) of a decimal number doesn't change the value of the number. 2,000 is bigger than 200, but 2.000 is the same as 2.00, 2.0 and even 2!

Connecting Fractions and Decimals

Decimals and fractions are the same thing — for real! The digits after a decimal point are just another way of showing numbers less than 1. Check this out:

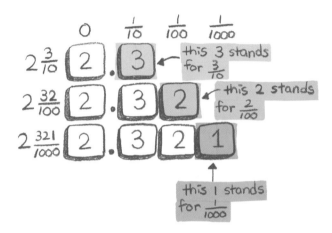

Tenths

If we put 2 ³⁄₁₀ into place-value columns, our whole number, 2, goes in the ones column, and the 3 goes in the tenths column to stand for ³⁄₁₀. So, we can totally just write 2 ³⁄₁₀ as 2.3.

Hundredths

We can do the same for 2 ³²⁄₁₀₀. Remember: put all the digits in their place-value columns and you'll see that we can write 2 ³²⁄₁₀₀ as 2.32.

Thousandths

Yep, the same thing happens with 2 ³²¹⁄₁₀₀₀. Just stick everything in their place-value columns and — ta-da! — it's the same as 2.321!

Turning Fractions into Decimals

Since fractions and decimals are different ways of writing the same thing, we can turn fractions into decimals. Rewriting fractions as decimals is easy — it takes only two simple steps. The key is to turn your fraction into an equivalent fraction whose denominator is either a tenth, hundredth or thousandth. If you don't quite get those, check out page 119 in Fractions.

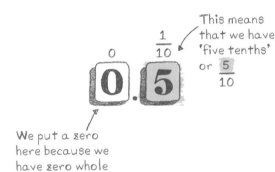

$$\frac{1}{2} = \frac{5}{10}$$

1×5

2×5

Q: How can we write ½ as a decimal?

Step 1: Take a look at the denominator, which is 2. Aha! That 2 goes into 10 evenly, so we're going to make 10 our new denominator. To get 2 to magically become 10, multiply it by 5. And remember, what we do to the bottom we have to do to the top, so multiply the numerator by 5 as well.

0 $\frac{1}{10}$

This means that we have 'five tenths' or $\frac{5}{10}$

0.5

We put a zero here because we have zero whole numbers

Step 2: Put ⁵⁄₁₀ into place-value columns. Stick a 5 in the tenths column, because you have five tenths, and voila! That's what ⁵⁄₁₀ looks like as a decimal.

A: ½ written as a decimal is 0.5.

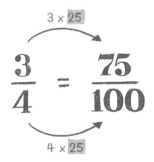

$$\frac{3}{4} = \frac{75}{100}$$

3×25

4×25

Q: How can we write ¾ as a decimal?

Step 1: Again, start with the denominator. Since 4 doesn't go into 10 evenly, let's try 100. It works! To turn 4 into 100, we multiply by 25. Do the same thing to the numerator.

Step 2: Now put ⁷⁵/₁₀₀ into place value columns. Put a 7 in the tenths column and a 5 in the hundredths column and ta-da!

This means that we have 'seventy five hundredths' or $\frac{75}{100}$

A: ¾ written as a decimal is 0.75.

Turning Decimals into Fractions

Rewriting decimals as fractions is easy! Just throw them over a multiple of 10. If it's a decimal number with one digit after the DP, put your decimal over 10. If it's two digits after the DP, it's 100. If it's three digits after the DP, it's 1000 ... super easy!

Q: How do we write 0.4 as a fraction?

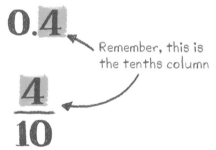

Remember, this is the tenths column

Step 1: Look at how many decimal places you've got. Here, there's just one, so we're dealing with tenths. Throw your number over a 10, and voila!

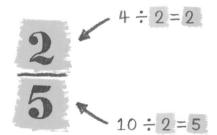

$4 \div 2 = 2$

$10 \div 2 = 5$

Step 2: We're not quite done. That fraction is not in it's simplest form. Simplify by dividing the top and bottom by 2 ... and ⅖ is your final answer.

A: 0.4 written as a fraction is ⅖.

Doing Actual Math with Decimals

We do math with decimals just like we do it with non-decimal numbers — it's easy if you remember to use place value.

Adding and Subtracting Decimals

No biggie! You add and subtract decimals the exact same way you do with whole numbers, using columns and place value.

Q: How do we add 7.5 + 2.43?

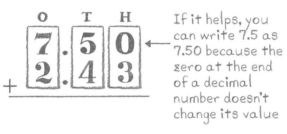

If it helps, you can write 7.5 as 7.50 because the zero at the end of a decimal number doesn't change its value

Step 1: Start by writing your decimals as usual, in their place-value columns. It's good to add zeros to the end of the decimal numbers so that everything's lined up nicely.

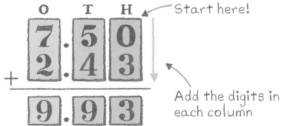

Start here!

Add the digits in each column

Step 2: Add as usual by adding up each column, starting at the far right. And there you go!

A: 7.5 + 2.43 = 9.93

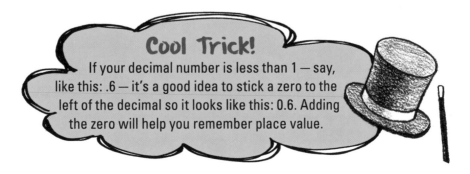

Cool Trick!
If your decimal number is less than 1 — say, like this: .6 — it's a good idea to stick a zero to the left of the decimal so it looks like this: 0.6. Adding the zero will help you remember place value.

141

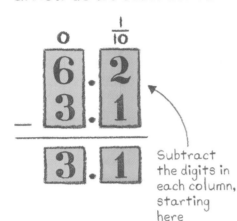

Step 1: Again, write your decimals in their place-value columns. You've got this!

Step 2: Subtract away, starting on the right, and working your way left.

Subtract the digits in each column, starting here

A: 6.2 – 3.1 = 3.1

Multiplying Decimals

This awesome hack will help you multiply decimals like a boss. All you need to do is forget the decimals even exist. Crazy! Multiply first, then add up the total number of decimal places in the factors. That's how many decimal places your actual answer will have.

Q: How do we multiply 0.3 x 1.2?

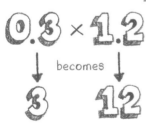

becomes

Step 1: Ditch the decimals and multiply the numbers as though they're totally normal whole numbers.

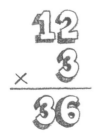

When multiplying with decimals, always move your decimal point to the left to get the final answer.

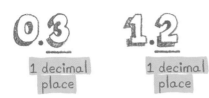

Step 2: Count how many decimal places each of your factors (0.3 and 1.2) had in the first place. Add their number of decimal places together. The total is how many decimal places your final answer will have.

1 decimal place + 1 decimal place = 2 decimal places

Final position of your decimal point

Start by drawing a pretend decimal point here. Now move it **two** place-values to the left!

Step 3: This is the fun part! Throw a pretend decimal point next to the last digit and step it to the left two times because we know our final answer will have two decimal places.

A: 0.3 x 1.2 = 0.36

Sometimes you'll see a decimal like 0.33333 where one digit or a sequence of digits (like 0.8181818181) repeats forever after the DP. This is called a **recurring decimal**. You can write these crazy decimals by putting a little line over the part that repeats, like $0.\overline{3}$ or $0.\overline{81}$. This means "Hey, that bit just keeps repeating, but I don't feel like writing it a million billion times."

So, what happens if you end up with more decimal places than actual digits?

Q: 0.03 x 1.2 =

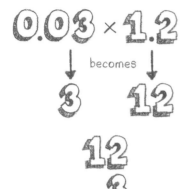

Step 1: Just like before, ditch the decimals and multiply like the pro you now are.

becomes

3   12

$$\begin{array}{r} 12 \\ \times\ 3 \\ \hline 36 \end{array}$$

Step 2: Count how many decimal places your original numbers have.

2 decimal places   1 decimal place

The answer will have 3 decimal places!

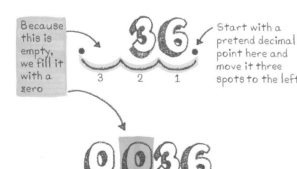

Because this is empty, we fill it with a zero

Start with a pretend decimal point here and move it three spots to the left

3 2 1

Step 3: Throw your pretend decimal point next to your last digit and step it to the left three times. But there are more decimal places than actual digits! Chill . . . just fill the empty space with a zero, and you are done.

A: 0.03 x 1.2 = 0.036

Dividing Decimals

Believe it or not, we get to use our old friend long division. It seems scary, but it's really not as bad as it sounds . . .

Dividing When the Dividend Is a Decimal

Seriously, there's nothing to it. Just write out your long division and divide as usual. It's mega-important to keep things perfectly lined up in their place-value columns so that your decimal point doesn't get confused about where to end up.

Q: 6.85 ÷ 5 =

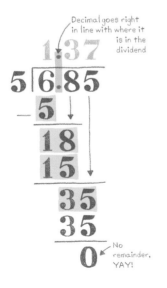

Decimal goes right in line with where it is in the dividend

No remainder, YAY!

Step 1: Put the decimal point on top of the division bracket RIGHT on top of where it is in your dividend and divide like the superstar that you are!

A: 6.85 ÷ 5 = 1.37

Dividing When the Divisor Is a Decimal

This also works when you're dividing a decimal by another decimal!

Q: 685 ÷ 0.5 = ?

Divisor has one decimal place, so the dividend needs one too.

Adding zeros after a decimal point on the end of a number doesn't change the number's value, so it's totally allowed!

Step 1: Put your dividend and divisor in their usual spots. Count the number of decimal places your divisor has. The dividend needs to have an equal or greater number of decimal places as the divisor. Since 0.5 has one decimal place, our dividend must have one too — so let's add one! It's all good because 685 and 685.0 are really the same thing.

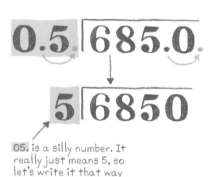

05. is a silly number. It really just means 5, so let's write it that way

Step 2: Look at your divisor and move the DP to the right as many times as it takes to turn it into a whole number. Here, we only need to do it once. But wait! You also must move the dividend's DP the same number of spots to the right.

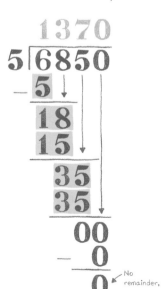

Step 3: And you're ready to divide away!

A: 685 ÷ 0.5 = 1370

No remainder, YAY!

PERCENTAGES

They're 100% Awesome!

What even are they? You know how decimals are another way to write fractions, right? Percentages are also just another way to write fractions! A percentage is a special fraction whose denominator is always 100. Why? Well, the word "percent" can be broken down into "per" and "cent." For those French speakers out there, "cent" means "hundred," so the word "percent" means "per hundred"! It shows an amount as part of 100. So, 10 percent just means 10 out of 100.

Sound familiar? Remember we learned that 10 out of 100 is called "ten hundredths"? You kind of already know this stuff — the only diff is that now we're going to call that same number "ten percent"!

Cool Trick!

We can use a percentage, decimal AND fraction to write the same number. For example:

$10\% = 0.10 = {}^{10}/_{100}$

Finding the Percentage of a Number

Use equivalent fractions here too — use what you already know!

Q: Find 40% of 500!

Step 1: First, think about what you're looking for. This question is basically saying, "Hey, 40 out of 100 equals SOMETHING out of 500 . . . Can you tell me what that something is?" So, set up your equivalent fractions like this:

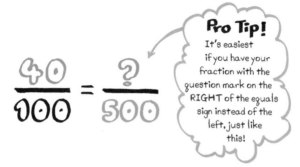

Pro Tip!
It's easiest if you have your fraction with the question mark on the RIGHT of the equals sign instead of the left, just like this!

Step 2: Now use the equivalent fraction hack to figure out what that big question mark in the numerator should be. We're trying to turn $^{40}/_{100}$ into an equivalent fraction whose denominator is 500, so all we do is figure out what we have to multiply 100 by to turn it into 500, and then just do the EXACT same thing to our numerator.

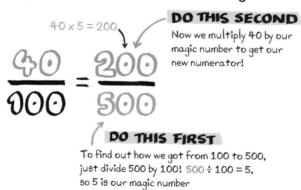

DO THIS SECOND
Now we multiply 40 by our magic number to get our new numerator!

$40 \times 5 = 200$

DO THIS FIRST
To find out how we got from 100 to 500, just divide 500 by 100! $500 \div 100 = 5$, so 5 is our magic number

A: Voila! 40% of 500 = 200.

Percentages, Decimals and Fractions Are Total BFFs!

Remember that percentages are another way of writing fractions, just like decimals are? Well, we can switch between percentages, decimals and fractions like total pros — check out this crazy awesome diagram for everything you need to know!

To turn a fraction into a decimal: divide the top by the bottom

$3 \div 5 = 0.6$

OR

Use equivalent fractions to turn your fraction into a denominator that is a multiple of 10

Fraction

$$\frac{3}{5}$$

To turn a percentage into a fraction, put your percentage over a denominator of 100 and then simplify.

$$\frac{60}{100} = \frac{3}{5}$$

To turn a decimal into a fraction, use place value to figure out your denominator, then simplify!

tenths

$0.6 = \frac{6}{10}$

$\frac{6}{10} = \frac{3}{5}$

To turn a fraction into a percentage, either use equivalent fractions to turn it into a fraction over 100 OR turn it into a decimal first and go from there!

Decimal

0.6

Percentage

60%

To turn a percentage into a decimal, divide by 100 (hint: move the decimal point two spots to the left!)

$60 \div 100 = 0.6$

To turn a decimal into a percentage, multiply the decimal by 100. (hint: just move the decimal point two spots to the right!)

$0.6 \times 100 = 60\%$

Don't forget to throw in the % sign!

Percentages, Decimals and Fractions: Super-Handy Conversion Chart!

Here's how it all relates, at a glance...

Picture!	Words!	Fraction!	Decimal!	Percentage!
	one tenth	1/10	0.1	10%
	one eight	1/8	0.125	12.5%
	one fifth	1/5	0.2	20%
	one quarter	1/4	0.25	25%
	three tenths	3/10	0.3	30%
	one third	1/3	0.333	33%
	two fifths	2/5	0.4	40%
	one half	1/2	0.5	50%
	three fifths	3/5	0.6	60%
	three quarters	3/4	0.75	75%
	seven eighths	7/8	0.875	87.5%
	ten tenths	10/10	1	100

It's 100% awesome!

Want MORE Math Hacks?

For more on calculating percentages, what a ratio is, the secret of BEDMAS, extra examples of questions and SO much more, visit: **www.scholastic.ca/math-hacks**

INDEX